THE SHOOTING SCRIPT ®

T H E

MATRIX

THE SHOOTING SCRIPT®

THE MATRIX

SCREENPLAY BY
LARRY & ANDY WACHOWSKI

FOREWORD BY WILLIAM GIBSON

A Newmarket Shooting Script® Series Book
NEWMARKET PRESS • NEW YORK

OTHER BOOKS IN THE NEWMARKET SHOOTING SCRIPT® SERIES INCLUDE:

*The Age of Innocence: The Shooting Script*A	*Man on the Moon: The Shooting Script*
American Beauty: The Shooting Script	*Nurse Betty: The Shooting Script*
The Birdcage: The Shooting Script	*The People vs. Larry Flynt: The Shooting Script*
Cast Away: The Shooting Script	*The Shawshank Redemption: The Shooting Script*
Dead Man Walking: The Shooting Script	*Snatch: The Shooting Script*
Erin Brockovich: The Shooting Script	*Snow Falling on Cedars: The Shooting Script*
'Gods and Monsters: The Shooting Script	*State and Main: The Shooting Script*
The Ice Storm: The Shooting Script	*Traffic: The Shooting Script*
Knight's Tale: The Shooting Script	*The Truman Show: The Shooting Script*

OTHER NEWMARKET PICTORIAL MOVIEBOOKS AND NEWMARKET INSIDER FILM BOOKS INCLUDE:

The Age of Innocence: A Portrait of the Film★	*The Jaws Log*
ALI: The Movie and The Man★	*Men in Black: The Script and the Story Behind the Film*★
Amistad: A Celebration of the Film by Steven Spielberg	*Neil Simon's Lost in Yonkers: The Illustrated Screenplay of the Film*★
The Art of The Matrix★	*Planet of The Apes: Re-imagined by Tim Burton*★
Bram Stoker's Dracula: The Film and the Legend★	*Saving Private Ryan: The Men, The Mission, The Movie*
Cradle Will Rock: The Movie and the Moment★	*The Sense and Sensibility Screenplay & Diaries*★
Crouching Tiger, Hidden Dragon: A Portrait of the Ang Lee Film★	*The Seven Years in Tibet Screenplay and Story*★
Dances with Wolves: The Illustrated Story of the Epic Film★	*Stuart Little: The Art, the Artists and the Story Behind the Amazing Movie*★
Gladiator: The Making of the Ridley Scott Epic Film	

★*Includes Screenplay*

CONTENTS

FOREWORD

WILLIAM GIBSON

I was afraid to see this movie. I was afraid because it was very popular, and friends told me it was very similar to my own work, and because it stars Keanu Reeves, who had starred in a film I had written. I was afraid that I would be jealous, or that I would resent the film's creators, or simply be unhappy. I had seen copies of the screenplay, and hadn't thought they promised a great deal, and Hollywood has generally done a very poor job around the theme of virtual reality.

The film had been in release, in America, for several weeks.

When I finally saw it, I only saw it because I found myself alone in an ocean hotel suite, in Santa Monica, and it was dark and cold and raining. My very good friend Roger came and rescued me, and insisted that I would like *The Matrix*. He dragged me out into the rain and his old VW Rabbit.

I knew then I would like *The Matrix*.

I liked it immediately, and liked it even more as the story unfolded. I felt a sense of excitement that I hadn't felt, watching a science fiction movie, in a very long time. The cynic in me kept waiting to be disappointed; waiting for the wrong move, the shabby explanation, the descent into the mess that Hollywood usually manages to make of a film like this. It never came, and when Neo soars at the end of the film, I went with him, in an innocent delight that I hadn't felt for quite a long time.

When I returned to Vancouver, I immediately took my fifteen-year-old daughter to see *The Matrix*. She had exactly the same misgivings. She loved it.

She loved it, I think, because it's something very special: a big, muscular, "effects" movie that's wildly generous with visual thrills, manages never to quit making sense (in the way an sf writer must demand that sf make sense), and, most important of all, has a good heart.

As I interpret it, *The Matrix* is a film about becoming conscious. It tells us that to become more conscious, to have the courage to seek that which is more real, is its own (and ultimately the greatest) reward. When Morpheus offers Neo the choice of the two pills, and Neo chooses (without knowing where it will take him, as indeed we never do) consciousness, we embark on a quest more primal than anything offered by *Star Wars*.

The ultimate goal in *The Matrix* is not the Force but the Real. When the film's Judas-figure betrays the heroes, he does so in order to be returned to illusion and denial, the false reality that Neo struggles to escape and overthrow.

American reviewers have interpreted this in Christian terms, seeing Neo as a Christ figure, but I prefer to see in him something more universal: a hero of the Real. I usually have a certain amount of trouble with the very idea of a hero, but in this case no: Keanu's Neo is my favorite-ever science fiction hero, absolutely.

William Gibson, 1999
Author of *Neuromancer, Virtual Light, Idoru, All Tomorrow's Parties*

THE SHOOTING SCRIPT

THE

MATRIX

THE MATRIX

Larry & Andy Wachowski

What follows is the shooting script for THE MATRIX, although it's not exactly what people saw in theaters. While everything that follows was filmed, changes occurred during editing. An example of this is in the final speech by Neo (scene 219) which was altered when test audiences didn't know the word "chrysalis." Other differences exist, from small cuts to dialogue tweaks. This is, however, the last draft before filming.

Shooting Script

August 12, 1998

FADE IN:

INT. COMPUTER SCREEN

On a computer screen; so close it has no boundaries.

A blinking cursor pulses in the electric darkness like a
heart coursing with phosphorous light, burning beneath the
derma of black-neon glass.

A phone begins to ring; we hear it as though we were making
the call. The cursor continues to throb, relentlessly
patient, until--

                    MAN (V.O.)
               Yeah?

Data now slashes across the screen, information flashing
faster than we can read:

                         SCREEN
               Call trans opt: received. 2-19-98
               13:24:18 REC:Log>.

                    WOMAN (V.O.)
               Is everything in place?

                         SCREEN
               Trace program: running.

We listen to the phone conversation as though we were on a
third line. The man's name is Cypher. The woman, Trinity.

                    TRINITY (WOMAN) (V.O.)
               I said, is everything in place?

The entire screen fills with racing columns of numbers.
Shimmering like green-electric rivers, they rush at a 10-
digit phone number in the top corner.

                    CYPHER (MAN) (V.O.)
               You weren't supposed to relieve
               me.

                    TRINITY (V.O.)
               I know, but I felt like taking a
               shift.

The area code is identified. The first three numbers
suddenly fixed, leaving only seven flowing columns.

                    CYPHER (V.O.)
               You like him, don't you? You like
               watching him?

We begin moving toward the screen, closing in as each digit is matched, one by one, snapping into place like the wheels of a slot machine.

> · TRINITY (V.O.)
> Don't be ridiculous.

> CYPHER (V.O.)
> We're going to kill him. Do you understand that? He's going to die just like the others.

> TRINITY (V.O.)
> Morpheus believes he is the One.

Only two thin digits left.

> CYPHER (V.O.)
> Do you?

> TRINITY (V.O.)
> I... it doesn't matter what I believe.

> CYPHER (V.O.)
> You don't, do you?

> TRINITY (V.O.)
> If you have something to say, I suggest you say it to Morpheus.

> CYPHER (V.O.)
> I intend to, believe me. Someone has to.

The final number pops into place--

> TRINITY (V.O.)
> Did you hear that?

> CYPHER (V.O.)
> Hear what?

> SCREEN
> Trace complete. Call origin: #312-555-0690.

> TRINITY (V.O.)
> Are you sure this line is clean?

> CYPHER (V.O.)
> Yeah, 'course I'm sure.

We move, still closer, the electric hum of the green numbers growing into an ominous roar.

>   TRINITY (V.O.)
>   I better go.

She hangs up as we pass through the numbers, entering the netherworld of the computer screen. Suddenly, a flashlight cuts open the darkness and we find ourselves in--

2   **INT. HEART O' THE CITY HOTEL - NIGHT**   2

The hotel was abandoned after a fire licked its way across the polyester carpeting, destroying several rooms as it spooled soot up the walls and ceiling, leaving patterns of permanent shadow.

We follow four armed POLICE OFFICERS using flashlights as they creep down the blackened hall and ready themselves on either side of Room 303.

The biggest of them violently kicks in the door. The other cops pour in behind him, guns thrust before them.

>   BIG COP
>   Police! Freeze!

The room is almost devoid of furniture. There is a fold-up table and chair with a phone, a modem, and a Powerbook computer. The only light in the room is the glow of the computer.

Sitting there, her hands still on the keyboard, is TRINITY, a woman in black leather.

>   BIG COP
>   Hands behind your head! Now! Do
>   it!

She slowly puts her hands behind her head.

3   **EXT. HEART O' THE CITY HOTEL - NIGHT**   3

A black sedan with tinted windows glides in through the police cruisers. AGENT SMITH, AGENT BROWN, and AGENT JONES get out of the car.

They wear dark suits and sunglasses even at night. They are also always hardwired; small Secret Service earphones in one ear, the cord coiling back into their shirt collars.

>   AGENT SMITH
>   Lieutenant?

> LIEUTENANT
> Oh shit.

> AGENT SMITH
> Lieutenant, you were given
> specific orders--

> LIEUTENANT
> I'm just doing my job. You gimme
> that Juris-my-dick-tion and you
> can cram it up your ass.

> AGENT SMITH
> The orders were for your
> protection.

The Lieutenant laughs.

> LIEUTENANT
> I think we can handle one little
> girl.

Agent Smith nods to Agent Brown as they start toward the
hotel.

> LIEUTENANT
> I sent two units. They're bringing
> her down now.

> AGENT SMITH
> No, Lieutenant, your men are
> already dead.

4   INT. HEART O' THE CITY HOTEL   4

The Big Cop flicks out his cuffs, the other cops holding a
bead. They've done this a hundred times, they know they've
got her, until the Big Cop reaches with the cuffs and Trinity
moves--

It almost doesn't register, so smooth and fast, inhumanly
fast.

The eye blinks and Trinity's palm snaps up and the nose
explodes, blood erupting. Her leg kicks with the force of a
wrecking ball and he flies back, a two-hundred-fifty-pound
sack of limp meat and bone that slams into the cop farthest
from her.

Trinity moves again, bullets raking the walls, flashlights
sweeping with panic as the remaining cops try to stop a
leather-clad ghost.

A gun still in the cop's hand is snatched, twisted, and fired. There is a final violent exchange of gunfire and when it's over, Trinity is the only one standing.

A flashlight rocks slowly to a stop.

> TRINITY
> Shit.

5   **EXT. HEART O' THE CITY HOTEL**   5

Agent Brown enters the hotel while Agent Smith heads for the alley.

6   **INT. HEART O' THE CITY HOTEL**   6

Trinity is on the phone, pacing. The other end is answered.

> MAN (V.O.)
> Operator.

> TRINITY
> Morpheus! The line was traced! I don't know how.

> MORPHEUS (MAN) (V.O.)
> I know. They cut the hardline. This line is not a viable exit.

> TRINITY
> Are there any Agents?

> MORPHEUS (V.O.)
> Yes.

> TRINITY
> Goddamnit!

> MORPHEUS (V.O.)
> You have to focus. There is a phone. Wells and Lake. You can make it.

She takes a deep breath, centering herself.

> TRINITY
> All right--

> MORPHEUS (V.O.)
> Go.

She drops the phone.

INT. HALL

She bursts out of the room as Agent Brown enters the hall,
leading another unit of police. Trinity races to the opposite
end, exiting through a broken window onto the fire escape.

EXT. FIRE ESCAPE

In the alley below, Trinity sees Agent Smith staring at her.
She can only go up.

EXT. ROOF

On the roof, Trinity is running as Agent Brown rises over the
parapet, leading the cops in pursuit.

Trinity begins to jump from one roof to the next, her
movements so clean, gliding in and out of each jump,
contrasted to the wild jumps of the cops.

Agent Brown, however, has the same unnatural grace.

The roof falls away into a wide back alley. The next building
is over 40 feet away but Trinity's face is perfectly calm,
staring at some point beyond the other roof.

                    COP
          That's it, we got her now.

The cops slow, realizing they are about to see something ugly
as Trinity drives at the edge, launching herself into the
air.

From above, the ground seems to flow beneath her as she hangs
in flight, then hits, somersaulting up, still running hard.

                    COP
          Jesus Christ--that's impossible!

They stare, slack-jawed, as Agent Brown duplicates the move
exactly, landing, rolling over a shoulder up onto one knee.

It is a dizzying chase up and over the dark plateaued
landscape of rooftops and sheer cliffs of brick. Ahead she
sees her only chance, 50 feet beyond the point where her path
drops away into a paved chasm, there is--

EXT. WINDOW

A window; a yellow glow in the midst of a dark brick
building.

Trinity zeros in on it, running as hard as she can and--

Hurtles herself into the empty night space, her body leveling into a dive. She falls, arms covering her head as the whole world seems to spin on its axis--

A10   INT. BACK STAIRWELL   A10

And she crashes with an explosion of glass and wood, then falls onto a back stairwell, tumbling, bouncing down stairs bleeding, broken--

But still alive.

She wheels on the smashed opening above, her gun instantly in her hand, trained, waiting for Agent Brown but is met by only a slight wind that hisses against the fanged maw of broken glass.

Trinity tries to move. Everything hurts.

                    TRINITY
              Get up, Trinity. You're fine. Get
              up--just get up!

She stands and limps down the rest of the stairs.

11   EXT. STREET   11

Trinity emerges from the shadows of an alley and, at the end of the block, in a pool of white street light, she sees it--

The telephone booth.

Obviously hurt, she starts down the concrete walk, focusing in completely, her pace quickening, as the phone begins to ring.

Across the street, a garbage truck suddenly turns U-turns, its tires screaming as it accelerates. Trinity sees the headlights of the truck arcing at the telephone booth as if taking aim.

Gritting through the pain, she races the truck, slamming into the booth, the headlights blindingly bright, bearing down on the box of Plexiglas just as--

She answers the phone.

There is a frozen instant of silence before the hulking mass of dark metal lurches up onto the sidewalk--

Barrelling through the booth, bulldozing it into a brick wall, smashing it to Plexiglas pulp.

After a moment, a black loafer steps down from the cab of the garbage truck. Agent Smith inspects the wreckage. There is no body. Trinity is gone.

His jaw sets as he grinds his molars in frustration. Agents Jones and Brown walk up behind him.

>   AGENT BROWN
>   She got out.

>   AGENT SMITH
>   It doesn't matter.

>   AGENT BROWN
>   The informant is real.

Agent Smith almost smiles.

>   AGENT SMITH
>   Yes.

>   AGENT JONES
>   We have the name of their next
>   target.

>   AGENT BROWN
>   The name is Neo.

The handset of the pay phone lays on the ground, separated in the crash like a severed limb.

>   AGENT SMITH
>   We'll need a search running.

>   AGENT JONES
>   It's already begun.

We are sucked towards the mouthpiece of the phone, closer and closer, until the smooth gray plastic spreads out like a horizon and the small holes widen until we fall through one--

Swallowed by darkness.

The darkness crackles with phosphorescent energy, the word "searching" blazing in around us as we emerge from a computer screen.

The screen flickers with windowing data as a search engine runs with a steady relentless rhythm.

We drift back from the screen and into--

12   INT. NEO'S APARTMENT   12

It is a studio apartment that seems overgrown with technology.

Weed-like cables coil everywhere, duct-taped into thickets
that wind up and around the legs of several desks. Tabletops
are filled with cannibalized equipment that lay open like an
autopsied corpse.

At the center of this technological rat-nest is NEO, a man
who knows more about living inside a computer than outside
one.

He is asleep in front of his PC. Behind him, the computer
screen suddenly goes blank. A prompt appears.

> SCREEN
> Wake up, Neo.

Neo's eye pries open. He sits up, one eye still closed,
looking around, unsure of where he is. He notices the screen.

He types "CTRL X" but the letter "T" appears.

> NEO
> What...?

He hits another and an "H" appears. He keeps typing, pushing
random functions and keys while the computer types out a
message as though it had a mind of its own.

He stops and stares at the four words on the screen.

> SCREEN
> The Matrix has you.

> NEO
> What the hell?

He hits the "ESC" button. Another message appears.

> SCREEN
> Follow the white rabbit.

He hits it again and the message repeats. He rubs his eyes
but when he opens them, there is another message.

> SCREEN
> Knock, knock, Neo.

Someone knocks on his door and he almost jumps out of his
chair. He looks back at the computer but the screen is now
blank.

Someone knocks again. Neo rises, still unnerved.

                    NEO
          Who is it?

                    CHOI (O.S.)
          It's Choi.

Neo flips a series of locks and opens the door, leaving the
chain on. A young Chinese MAN stands with several of his
friends.

                    NEO
          You're two hours late.

                    CHOI
          I know. It's her fault.

                    NEO
          You got the money?

                    CHOI
          Two grand.

He takes out an envelope and gives it to Neo through the
cracked door.

                    NEO
          Hold on.

He closes the door. On the floor near his bed is a book,
Baudrillard's Simulacra and Simulations. The book has been
hollowed out and inside are several computer disks. He takes
one, sticks the money in the book and drops it on the floor.

Opening the door, he hands the disk to Choi.

                    CHOI
          Hallelujah! You are my savior,
          man! My own personal Jesus Christ!

                    NEO
          If you get caught using that--

                    CHOI
          I know, I know. This never
          happened. You don't exist.

                    NEO
          Right...

Neo nods as the strange feeling of unrealness suddenly
returns.

                    CHOI
          Something wrong, man? You look a
          little whiter than usual.

                    NEO
          I don't know... My computer...

He looks back at Choi, unable to explain what just happened.

                    NEO
          You ever have the feeling that
          you're not sure if you're awake or
          still dreaming?

                    CHOI
          All the time. It's called
          mescaline and it is the only way
          to fly.

He smiles and slaps the hand of his nearest droog.

                    CHOI
          It sounds to me like you need to
          unplug, man. A little R and R.
          What do you think, Dujour, should
          we take him with us?

                    DUJOUR
          Definitely.

                    NEO
          I can't. I have to work tomorrow.

                    DUJOUR
          Come on. It'll be fun. I promise.

He looks up at her and suddenly notices on her black leather
motorcycle jacket dozens of pins: bands, symbols, slogans,
military medals and--

A small white rabbit. The room tilts.

                    NEO
          Yeah, yeah. Sure, I'll go.

13   INT. APARTMENT   13

An older apartment; a series of halls connects a chain of
small high-ceilinged rooms lined with heavy casements.

Smoke hangs like a veil, blurring the few lights there are.

Dressed predominantly in black, people are everywhere,
gathered in cliques around pieces of furniture like jungle
cats around a tree.

Neo stands against a wall, alone, sipping from a bottle of
beer; feeling completely out of place, he is about to leave
when he notices a woman staring at him.

The woman is Trinity. She walks straight up to him.

In the nearest room, shadow-like figures grind against each
other to the pneumatic beat of industrial music.

>   TRINITY
>   Hello, Neo.

>   NEO
>   How do you know that name?

>   TRINITY
>   I know a lot about you. I've been
>   wanting to meet you for some time.

>   NEO
>   Who are you?

>   TRINITY
>   My name is Trinity.

>   NEO
>   Trinity? The Trinity? The Trinity
>   that cracked the I.R.S. D-Base?

>   TRINITY
>   That was a long time ago.

>   NEO
>   Gee-zus.

>   TRINITY
>   What?

>   NEO
>   I just thought... you were a guy.

>   TRINITY
>   Most guys do.

Neo is a little embarrassed.

>   NEO
>   Do you want to go somewhere and
>   talk?

                    TRINITY
          No. It's safe here and I don't
          have much time.

The music is so loud they must stand very close, talking
directly into each other's ear.

                    NEO
          That was you on my computer?

She nods.

                    NEO
          How did you do that?

                    TRINITY
          Right now, all I can tell you, is
          that you are in danger. I brought
          you here to warn you.

                    NEO
          Of what?

                    TRINITY
          They're watching you, Neo.

                    NEO
          Who is?

                    TRINITY
          Please. Just listen. I know why
          you're here, Neo. I know what
          you've been doing. I know why you
          hardly sleep, why you live alone
          and why, night after night, you
          sit at your computer; you're
          looking for him.

Her body is against his; her lips very close to his ear.

                    TRINITY
          I know because I was once looking
          for the same thing, but when he
          found me he told me I wasn't
          really looking for him. I was
          looking for an answer.

There is a hypnotic quality to her voice and Neo feels the
words, like a drug, seeping into him.

                    TRINITY
          It's the question that drives us, the
          question that brought you here. You
          know the question just as I did.

                              NEO
                    What is the Matrix?

                              TRINITY
                    When I asked him, he said that no
                    one could ever be told the answer
                    to that question. They have to see
                    it to believe it.

She leans close, her lips almost touching his ear.

                              TRINITY
                    The answer is out there, Neo. It's
                    looking for you and it will find
                    you, if you want it to.

She turns and he watches her melt into the shifting wall of
bodies.

A sound rises steadily, growing out of the music, pressing in
on Neo until it is all he can hear as we cut to--

14   **INT. NEO'S APARTMENT**   14

The sound is an alarm clock, slowly dragging Neo to
consciousness. He strains to read the clock-face: 9:15AM.

                              NEO
                    Shitshitshit.

15   **EXT. SKYSCRAPER**   15

The downtown office of Meta CorTechs, a software development
company.

16   **INT. META CORTECHS OFFICE**   16

The main offices are along each wall, the windows overlooking
downtown. RHINEHEART, the ultimate company man, lectures Neo
without looking at him, typing at his computer continuously.

Neo stares at two window cleaners on a scaffolding outside,
dragging their rubber squeegees down the surface of the
glass.

                              RHINEHEART
                    You have a problem with authority,
                    Mr. Anderson.You believe that you
                    are special, that somehow the rules
                    do not apply to you. Obviously,
                    you are mistaken.

His long, bony fingers resume clicking the keyboard.

                    RHINEHEART
          This company is one of the top
          software companies in the world
          because every single employee
          understands that they are part of
          a whole. Thus, if an employee has
          a problem, the company has a
          problem.

He turns again.

                    RHINEHEART
          The time has come to make a
          choice, Mr. Anderson. Either you
          choose to be at your desk on time
          from this day forth, or you choose
          to find yourself another job. Do I
          make myself clear?

                    NEO
          Yes, Mr. Rhineheart. Perfectly
          clear.

17   **INT. NEO'S CUBICLE**   17

The entire floor looks like a human honeycomb, with a
labyrinth of cubicles structured around a core of elevators.

                    VOICE (O.S.)
          Thomas Anderson?

Neo turns and finds a FEDERAL EXPRESS GUY at his cubicle
door.

                    NEO
          Yeah. That's me.

Neo signs the electronic pad and the Fedex Guy hands him the
softpak.

                    FEDEX GUY
          Have a nice day.

He opens the bag. Inside is a cellular phone. It seems the
instant it is in his hand, it rings. Unnerved, he flips it
open.

                    NEO
          Hello?

                    MORPHEUS (V.O.)
          Hello, Neo. Do you know who this
          is?

Neo's knees give and he sinks into his chair.

                    NEO
               Morpheus...

                    MORPHEUS (V.O.)
               I've been looking for you, Neo. I
               don't know if you're ready to see
               what I want to show you, but
               unfortunately, we have run out of
               time. They're coming for you, Neo.
               And I'm not sure what they're
               going to do.

                    NEO
               Who's coming for me?

                    MORPHEUS (V.O.)
               Stand up and see for yourself.

                    NEO
               Right now?

                    MORPHEUS (V.O.)
               Yes. Now.

Neo starts to stand.

                    MORPHEUS (V.O.)
               Do it slowly. The elevator.

His head peeks up over the partition. At the elevator, he
sees Agent Smith, Agent Brown, and Agent Jones leading a
group of cops. A female employee turns and points out Neo's
cubicle.

Neo ducks.

                    NEO
               Holy shit!

                    MORPHEUS (V.O.)
               Yes.

One cop stays at the elevator, the others follow the Agents.

                    NEO
               What the hell do they want with
               me?!

                    MORPHEUS (V.O.)
               I'm not sure, but if you don't
               want to find out, you better get
               out of there.

                    NEO
          How?!

                    MORPHEUS (V.O.)
          I can guide you out, but you have
          to do exactly what I say.

The Agents are moving quickly towards the cubicle.

                    MORPHEUS (V.O.)
          The cubicle across from you is
          empty.

                    NEO
          But what if...?

                    MORPHEUS (V.O.)
          Go! Now!

Neo lunges across the hall, diving into the other cubicle
just as the Agents turn into his row.

Neo crams himself into a dark corner, clutching the phone
tightly to him.

                    MORPHEUS (V.O.)
          Stay here for a moment.

The Agents enter Neo's empty cubicle. A cop is sent to search
the bathroom.

Morpheus's voice is a whisper in Neo's ear.

                    MORPHEUS (V.O.)
          A little longer...

Brown is talking to another employee.

                    MORPHEUS (V.O.)
          When I tell you, go to the end of
          the row to the first office on the
          left, stay as low as you can.

Sweat trickles down his forehead.

                    MORPHEUS (V.O.)
          Now.

Neo rolls out of the cubicle, his eyes popping as he freezes
right behind a cop who has just turned around.

Staying crouched, he sneaks away down the row, shooting
across the opening to the first office on the left.

The room is empty.

>   MORPHEUS (V.O.)
>   Good. Outside there is a scaffold.

>   NEO
>   How do you know all this?

Morpheus laughs quietly.

>   MORPHEUS (V.O.)
>   The answer is coming, Neo. There
>   is a window in front of you. Open
>   it.

He opens the window. The wind howls into the room.

>   MORPHEUS (V.O.)
>   You can use the scaffold to get to
>   the roof.

>   NEO
>   No! It's too far away.

>   MORPHEUS (V.O.)
>   There's a ledge. It's a short
>   climb. You can make it.

Neo looks down; the building's glass wall vertigos into a
concrete chasm.

>   NEO
>   No way, no way, this is crazy.

>   MORPHEUS (V.O.)
>   There are only two ways out of
>   this building. One is that
>   scaffold. The other is in their
>   custody. You take a chance either
>   way. I leave it to you.

Click. He hangs up. Neo looks at the door, then back at the
scaffold.

>   NEO
>   This is insane! Why is this
>   happening to me? What did I do?
>   I'm nobody. I didn't do anything.

He climbs up onto the window ledge. Hanging onto the frame, he steps onto the small ledge. The scaffold seems even farther away.

> NEO
> I'm going to die.

The wind suddenly blasts up the face of the building, knocking Neo off balance. Recoiling, he clings harder to the frame, and the phone falls out of his hand.

He watches as it is swallowed by the distance beneath him.

> NEO
> This is insane! I can't do this!
> Forget it!

He climbs back into the office just as a cop opens the door.

> NEO
> Shit!

19   **EXT. SKYSCRAPER**   19

The Agents lead a handcuffed Neo out of the revolving doors, forcing his head down as they push him into the dark sedan.

Trinity watches in the rear view mirror of her motorcycle.

> TRINITY
> Shit.

20   **INT. INTERROGATION ROOM**   20

Close on a camera monitor; wide angle view of a white room where Neo is sitting at a table alone. We move into the monitor, entering the room as if the monitor was a window.

At the same moment, the door opens and the Agents enter. Agent Smith sits down across from Neo. A thick manila envelope slaps down on the table. The name on the file: "Anderson, Thomas A."

> AGENT SMITH
> As you can see, we've had our eye
> on you for some time now, Mr.
> Anderson.

He opens the file. Paper rattle marks the silence as he flips several pages. Neo cannot tell if he is looking at the file or at him.

                    AGENT SMITH
            It seems that you have been living
            two lives. In one life, you are
            Thomas A. Anderson, program writer
            for a respectable software
            company. You have a social
            security number, you pay your
            taxes, and you help your landlady
            carry out her garbage.

The pages continue to turn.

                    AGENT SMITH
            The other life is lived in
            computers where you go by the
            hacker alias Neo, and are guilty
            of virtually every computer crime
            we have a law for.

Neo feels himself sinking into a pit of shit.

                    AGENT SMITH
            One of these lives has a future.
            One of them does not.

He closes the file.

                    AGENT SMITH
            I'm going to be as forthcoming as
            I can be, Mr. Anderson. You are
            here because we need your help.

He removes his sunglasses; his eyes are an unnatural ice-
blue.

                    AGENT SMITH
            We know that you have been
            contacted by a certain individual.
            A man who calls himself Morpheus.
            Whatever you think you know about
            this man is irrelevant. The fact
            is that he is wanted for acts of
            terrorism in more countries than
            any other man in the world. He is
            considered by many authorities to
            be the most dangerous man alive.

He leans closer.

                    AGENT SMITH
            My colleagues believe that I am
            wasting my time with you but I
            believe you want to do the right
            thing.
                        (MORE)

                    AGENT SMITH (cont'd)
               It is obvious that you are
               an intelligent man, Mr. Anderson,
               and that you are interested in the
               future. That is why I believe you
               are ready to put your past
               mistakes behind you and get on
               with your life.

Neo tries to match his stare.

                    AGENT SMITH
               We are willing to wipe the slate
               clean, to give you a fresh start
               and all we are asking in return is
               your cooperation in bringing a
               known terrorist to justice.

Neo nods to himself.

                    NEO
               Yeah. Wow. That sounds like a real
               good deal. But I think I have a
               better one. How about I give you
               the finger--

He does.

                    NEO
               And you give me my phone call!

Agent Smith puts his glasses back on.

                    AGENT SMITH
               You disappoint me, Mr. Anderson.

                    NEO
               You can't scare me with this
               Gestapo crap. I know my rights. I
               want my phone call!

Agent Smith smiles.

                    AGENT SMITH
               And tell me, Mr. Anderson, what
               good is a phone call if you are
               unable to speak?

The question unnerves Neo and strangely he begins to feel the
muscles in his jaw tighten. The standing Agents snicker,
watching Neo's confusion grow into panic.

Neo feels his lips grow soft and sticky as they slowly seal shut, melding into each other until all traces of his mouth are gone.

Wild with fear, he lunges for the door but the Agents restrain him, holding him in the chair.

> AGENT SMITH
> You are going to help us, Mr.
> Anderson, whether you want to or
> not.

Smith nods and the other two rip open his shirt. From a case taken out of his suit coat, Smith removes a long, fiber-optic wire tap.

Neo struggles helplessly as Smith dangles the wire over his exposed abdomen. Horrified, he watches as the electronic device animates, becoming an organic creature that resembles a hybrid of an insect and a fluke worm.

Thin, whisker-like tendrils reach out and probe into Neo's navel. He bucks wildly as Smith drops the creature which looks for a moment like an uncut umbilical cord--

Before it begins to burrow, its tail thrashing as it worms its way inside.

21   **INT. NEO'S APARTMENT - NIGHT**   21

Screaming, Neo bolts upright in bed.

He realizes that he is home. Was it a dream? His mouth is normal. His stomach looks fine. He starts to take a deep, everything-is-okay breath when--

The phone rings.

It almost stops his heart. It continues ringing, building pressure in the room, forcing him up out of bed, sucking him in with an almost gravitational force. He answers it, saying nothing.

> MORPHEUS (V.O.)
> This line is tapped so I must be
> brief.

> NEO
> The Agents--

> MORPHEUS (V.O.)
> They got to you first, but they've
> underestimated how important you
> are. If they knew what I know, you
> would probably be dead.

                    NEO
          What are you talking about? What
          the hell is happening to me?

                    MORPHEUS
          You're the One, Neo. You see, you
          may have spent the last few years
          looking for me, but I've spent
          most of my life looking for you.

Neo feels sick.

                    MORPHEUS (V.O.)
          Do you still want to meet?

                    NEO
          ...yes.

                    MORPHEUS (V.O.)
          Go to the Adams Street bridge.

Click. He closes his eyes, unsure of what he has done.

22   **EXT. CITY STREET - NIGHT**   22

       It is just beyond the middle of the night, that time when it
       seems there are no rules and everything feels unsafe. Neo's
       boots scrape against the concrete. Every pair of eyes he
       passes seems to follow him. Rain pours from a black sky.

       As he reaches the bridge, headlights creep in behind him. He
       turns just as the car slides quickly to a stop beside him.
       The back door opens.

                    TRINITY
          Get in.

23   **INT. CAR**   23

       A large man named APOC is driving. Beside him is a beautiful
       androgyne called SWITCH, aiming a large gun at Neo. Window
       wipers beat heavily against the windshield.

                    NEO
          What the hell is this?!

                    TRINITY
          It's necessary, Neo. For our
          protection.

                    NEO
          From what?

                    TRINITY
          From you.

She lifts a strange steel and glass device that looks like a cross between a rib separator, speculum, and air compressor.

> SWITCH
> Take off your shirt.

He looks at the strange device and the gun still trained on him.

> NEO
> What? Why?

> SWITCH
> Stop the car.

Apoc does.

> SWITCH
> Listen to me, coppertop. We don't
> have time for 'twenty questions.'
> Right now there is only one rule.
> Our way or the highway.

> NEO
> Fine.

Neo opens the door.

> TRINITY
> Neo, please, you have to trust me.

> NEO
> Why?

> TRINITY
> Because you've been down there,
> Neo. You already know that road.
> You know exactly where it ends.

Neo stares out into sheets of rain railing against the dark street beyond the open door.

> TRINITY
> And I know that's not where you
> want to be.

He closes the door.

A23   **EXT. DARK STREET**   A23

A moment later the green street lights curve over the car's tinted windshield as it rushes through the wet underworld.

Neo grudgingly strips off his T-shirt.

>   TRINITY
>   Lie back.

Trinity aims the device at Neo, its glass snout forming a
seal over his navel. Switch snaps a cable into the front seat
cigarette lighter.

>   NEO
>   What is this thing?

>   TRINITY
>   We think you're bugged. Try to
>   relax.

She turns a dial and the machine bears down on Neo's
midsection, the cylinder sucking hard at his stomach.

Neo screams, squinting in pain as Trinity watches the needle
on a pressure gauge climb steadily.

>   TRINITY
>   Come on, come on...

On a small monitor that projects an ultrasound-like image, we
see Neo's insides begin to slither and churn. He gasps as
something wiggles beneath his skin inside his stomach.

>   SWITCH
>   It's on the move.

>   TRINITY
>   Shit.

>   SWITCH
>   You're gonna lose it.

>   TRINITY
>   No I'm not. Clear.

The forboding word hangs in Neo's ear for a moment when
Trinity squeezes a trigger. Electric current hammers into Neo
and rigid convulsions take hold of him beneath the flickering
car lamp until--

Something finally rockets wetly out of Neo's stomach through
the extractor's coils.

>   NEO
>   Jesus Christ! It's real?! That
>   thing is real?!

Trinity lifts a glass cage at the end of the tubing. Inside the small fluke-like bug flips and squirms, its tendrils flapping against the clear walls.

She unrolls the window and dumps it out.

| 25 | **EXT. CAR** | 25 |

It hits the pavement with a metallic tink, reverted back into a common wire tap, as the car disappears into the rainy night.

| 26 | **EXT. HOTEL LAFAYETTE** | 26 |

The car stops in a deserted alley behind a forgotten hotel.

| 27 | **INT. HOTEL LAFAYETTE** | 27 |

It is a place of putrefying elegance, a rotting host of urban maggotry.

Trinity leads Neo from the stairwell down the hall of the thirteenth floor. They stop outside room 1313.

> TRINITY
> This is it.

Neo can hear his own heart pounding.

> TRINITY
> Let me give one piece of advice.
> Be honest. He knows more than you
> can possibly imagine.

| 28 | **INT. ROOM 1313** | 28 |

Across the room, a DARK FIGURE stares out the tall windows veiled with decaying lace.

He turns and his smile lights up the room. A dull roar of thunder shakes the old building.

> MORPHEUS
> At last.

He wears a long black coat and his eyes are invisible behind circular mirrored glasses. He strides to Neo and they shake hands.

> MORPHEUS
> Welcome, Neo. As you no doubt have
> guessed, I am Morpheus.

> NEO
> It's an honor.

                    MORPHEUS
          No, the honor is mine. Please.
          Come. Sit.

He nods to Trinity and she exits through a door to an
adjacent room. They sit across from one another in cracked,
burgundy-leather chairs.

                    MORPHEUS
          I imagine, right now, you must be
          feeling a bit like Alice, tumbling
          down the rabbit hole?

                    NEO
          You could say that.

                    MORPHEUS
          I can see it in your eyes. You
          have the look of a man who accepts
          what he sees because he is
          expecting to wake up.

A smile, razor-thin, curls the corner of his lips.

                    MORPHEUS
          Ironically, this is not far from
          the truth. But I'm getting ahead
          of myself. Can you tell me, Neo,
          why are you here?

                    NEO
          You're Morpheus, you're a legend.
          Most hackers would die to meet
          you.

                    MORPHEUS
          Yes. Thank you. But I think we
          both know there's more to it than
          that. Do you believe in fate, Neo?

                    NEO
          No.

                    MORPHEUS
          Why not?

                    NEO
          Because I don't like the idea that
          I'm not in control of my life.

                    MORPHEUS
          I know exactly what you mean.

Again, that smile that could cut glass.

              MORPHEUS
          Let me tell you why you are here.
          You have come because you know
          something. What you know you can't
          explain but you feel it. You've
          felt it your whole life, felt that
          something is wrong with the world.
          You don't know what, but it's
          there like a splinter in your
          mind, driving you mad. It is this
          feeling that brought you to me. Do
          you know what I'm talking about?

              NEO
          The Matrix?

              MORPHEUS
          Do you want to know what it is?

Neo swallows hard and nods.

              MORPHEUS
          The Matrix is everywhere, it's all
          around us, here even in this room.
          You can see it out your window or
          on your television. You feel it when
          you go to work, or go to church or
          pay your taxes. It is the world that
          has been pulled over your eyes to
          blind you from the truth.

              NEO
          What truth?

              MORPHEUS
          That you are a slave, Neo. Like
          everyone else, you were born into
          bondage, kept inside a prison that
          you cannot smell, taste, or touch.
          A prison for your mind.

The leather creaks as he leans back.

              MORPHEUS
          Unfortunately, no one can be told
          what the Matrix is. You have to
          see it for yourself.

Morpheus opens his hands. In the right is a red pill. In the
left, a blue pill.

                  MORPHEUS
        This is your last chance. After
        this, there is no going back. You
        take the blue pill and the story
        ends. You wake in your bed and you
        believe whatever you want to
        believe.

The pills in his open hands are reflected in the glasses.

                  MORPHEUS
        You take the red pill and you stay
        in Wonderland and I show you how
        deep the rabbit hole goes.

Neo feels the smooth skin of the capsules, the moisture
growing in his palms.

                  MORPHEUS
        Remember that all I am offering is
        the truth. Nothing more.

Neo opens his mouth and swallows the red pill. The Cheshire
smile returns.

                  MORPHEUS
        Follow me.

29   **INT. OTHER ROOM**   **29**

He leads Neo into the other room, which is cramped with high-
tech equipment, glowing ash-blue and electric green from the
racks of monitors. Trinity, Apoc, Switch, and Cypher look up
as they enter.

                  MORPHEUS
        Apoc, are we on-line?

                  APOC
        Almost.

He and Trinity are working quickly, hard-wiring a complex
system of monitors, modules, and drives.

                  MORPHEUS
        Neo, time is always against us.
        Will you take a seat there?

Neo sits in a chair in the center of the room and Trinity
begins gently fixing white electrode disks to him. Near the
chair is an old oval dressing mirror that is cracked. He
whispers to Trinity:

                    NEO
             You did all this?

She nods, placing a set of headphones over his ears. They are
wired to an old hotel phone.

                    MORPHEUS
             The pill you took is part of a
             trace program. It's designed to
             disrupt your input/output carrier
             signal so we can pinpoint your
             location.

                    NEO
             What does that mean?

                    CYPHER
             It means buckle up, Dorothy,
             'cause Kansas is going bye-bye.

Distantly, through the ear phones, he hears Apoc pounding on
a keyboard. Sweat beads his face. His eyes blink and twitch
when he notices the mirror.

Wide-eyed, he stares as it begins to heal itself, a webwork
of cracks that slowly run together as though the mirror were
becoming liquid.

                    NEO
             Did you...?

Cypher works with Apoc, checking reams of phosphorescent
data. Trinity monitors Neo's electric vital signs. Neo
reaches out to touch the mirror and his fingers disappear
beneath the rippling surface.

Quickly, he tries to pull his fingers out but the mirror
stretches in long rubbery strands like mirrored-taffy stuck
to his fingertips.

                    MORPHEUS
             Have you ever had a dream, Neo,
             that you were so sure was real?

A flash of lightning flickers white hot against Neo.

                    NEO
             This can't be...

                    MORPHEUS
             Be what? Be real?

The strands thin like rubber cement as he pulls away, until
the fragile wisps of mirror thread break.

                  MORPHEUS
        What if you were unable to wake
        from that dream, Neo? How would
        you know the difference between
        the dream world and the real
        world?

Neo looks at his hand; fingers distended into mirrored
icicles that begin to melt rapidly, dripping, running like
wax down his fingers, spreading across his palm where he sees
his face reflected.

                  NEO
        Uh-oh...

                  TRINITY
        It's going into replication.

                  MORPHEUS
        Apoc?

                  APOC
        Still nothing.

Morpheus takes out a cellular phone and dials a number.

                  MORPHEUS
        Tank, we're going to need the
        signal soon.

The mirror gel seems to come to life, racing, crawling up his
arms like hundreds of insects.

The mirror creeps up his neck as Neo begins to panic, tipping
his head as though he were sinking into the mirror, trying to
keep his mouth up.

                  NEO
        It's cold.

                  TRINITY
        I got a fibrillation!

                  MORPHEUS
        Shit! Apoc?

Streams of mercury run from Neo's nose.

                  APOC
        Targeting... almost there.

An alarm on Trinity's monitor erupts.

                    TRINITY
              He's going into arrest!

                    APOC
              Lock! I got him!

                    MORPHEUS
              Now, Tank, now!

His eyes tear with mirror, rolling up and closing as a high-
pitched electric scream erupts in the headphones. It is a
piercing shriek like a computer calling to another computer--

Neo's body arches in agony and we are pulled like we were
pulled into the holes of the phone, sucked into his scream
and swallowed by darkness.

30   INT. POWER PLANT   30

Close on a man's body floating in a womb-red amnion. His body
spasms, fighting against the thick gelatin.

Metal tubes, surreal versions of hospital tubes, obscure his
face. Other lines like IVs are connected to limbs and cover
his genitals.

He is struggling desperately now. Air bubbles into the Jell-O
but does not break the surface. Pressing up, the surface
distends, stretching like a red rubber cocoon.

Unable to breathe, he fights wildly to stand, clawing at the
thinning elastic shroud, until it ruptures, a hole widening
around his mouth as he sucks for air. Tearing himself free,
he emerges from the cell.

It is Neo.

He is bald and naked, his body slick with gelatin. Dizzy,
nauseous, he waits for his vision to focus.

He is standing in an oval capsule of clear alloy filled with
red gelatin, the surface of which has solidified like curdled
milk. The IVs in his arms are plugged into outlets that
appear to be grafted to his flesh.

He feels the weight of another cable and reaches to the back
of his head where he finds an enormous coaxial plugged and
locked into the base of his skull. He tries to pull it out
but it would be easier to pull off a finger.

To either side he sees other tube-shaped pods filled with red
gelatin; beneath the wax-like surface, pale and motionless,
he sees other human beings.

Fanning out in a circle, there are more. All connected to a center core, each capsule like a red, dimly glowing petal attached to a black metal stem.

Above him, level after level, the stem rises seemingly forever. He moves to the foot of the capsule and looks out. The image assaults his mind.

Towers of glowing petals spiral up to incomprehensible heights, disappearing down into a dim murk like an underwater abyss.

His sight is blurred and warped, exaggerating the intensity of the vision. The sound of the plant is like the sound of the ocean heard from inside the belly of Leviathan.

From above, a machine drops directly in front of Neo. He swallows his scream as it seems to stare at him. It is almost insect-like in its design; beautiful housings of alloyed metal covering organic-like systems of hard and soft polymers.

The machine seizes hold of Neo, paralyzing him as the cable lock at the back of his neck spins and opens.

The cable disengages itself. A long clear plastic needle and cerebrum-chip slides from the anterior of Neo's skull with an ooze of blood and spinal fluid. The other connective hoses snap free and snake away as the machine lets Neo go.

Suddenly, the back of the unit opens and a tremendous vacuum, like an airplane door opening, sucks the gelatin and then Neo into a black hole.

31   INT. WASTE LINE   31

The pipe is a waste disposal system and Neo falls, sliding with the clot of gelatin.

Banking through pipe spirals and elbows, flushing up through grease traps clogged with oily clumps of cellulite.

32   INT. SEWER MAIN   32

Neo begins to drown when he is suddenly snatched from the flow of waste.

The metallic cable then lifts, pulling him up into the belly of the futuristic flying machine hovering inside the sewer main.

33   INT. HOVERCRAFT   33

The metal harness opens and drops the half-conscious Neo onto the floor. Human hands and arms help him up as he finds himself looking straight at Morpheus.

He smiles.

>   MORPHEUS
> Welcome to the real world, Neo.

Neo passes out.

>   FADE TO BLACK.

34   **INT. HOVERCRAFT**   34

We have no sense of time. We hear voices whispering.

>   MORPHEUS
> We've done it, Trinity. We found
> him.

>   TRINITY
> I hope you're right.

>   MORPHEUS
> I don't have to hope it. I know
> it.

Neo's eyes flutter open. We see Morpheus' face above us,
angelic in the fluorescent glow of a light stick.

>   NEO (O.S.)
> ...am I dead?

>   MORPHEUS
> Far from it.

>   FADE TO BLACK.

35   **INT. HOVERCRAFT - INFIRMARY**   35

He opens his eyes again, something tingling through him. He
focuses and sees his body pierced with dozens of acupuncture-
like needles wired to a strange device.

>   DOZER
> He still needs a lot of work.

DOZER and Morpheus are operating on Neo.

>   NEO
> What are you doing?

>   MORPHEUS
> Your muscles have atrophied. We're
> rebuilding them.

Fluorescent light sticks burn unnaturally bright.

>   NEO
>   Why do my eyes hurt?

>   MORPHEUS
>   You've never used them before.

Morpheus closes Neo's eyes and Neo lays back.

>   MORPHEUS
>   Rest, Neo. The answers are coming.

36   INT. NEO'S ROOM   36

Neo wakes up from a deep sleep, feeling better. He begins to
examine himself. There is a futuristic IV plugged into the
jack in his forearm. He pulls it out, staring at the grafted
outlet.

He runs his hand over the short hair now covering his head.
His fingers find and explore the large outlet in the base of
his skull.

Just as he starts to come unglued, Morpheus opens the door.

>   NEO
>   Morpheus, what's happened to me?
>   What is this place?

>   MORPHEUS
>   More important than what is when?

>   NEO
>   When?

>   MORPHEUS
>   You believe the year is 1997 when
>   in fact it is much closer to 2197.
>   I can't say for certain what year
>   it is because we honestly do not
>   know.

The wind is knocked from Neo's chest.

>   MORPHEUS
>   There is no reason for me to try
>   to explain it when I can simply
>   show it. Come with me.

37   INT. HOVERCRAFT   37

Like a sleepwalker, Neo follows Morpheus through the ship.

MORPHEUS
                        MORPHEUS
            This is my ship, the
            Nebuchadnezzar. It's a hovercraft.
            Small like a submarine. It's
            cramped and cold. But it's home.

They climb a ladder up to the main deck.

38   **INT. MAIN DECK**   38

Everyone is there.

                        MORPHEUS
            This is the main deck. You know
            most of my crew.

Trinity smiles and nods.

                        MORPHEUS
            The ones you don't know. That's
            Mouse, Cypher, and Switch. Those
            two guys are Tank and Dozer.

The names and faces wash meaninglessly over Neo.

                        MORPHEUS
            And this, this is the Core. This
            is where we broadcast our pirate
            signal and hack into the Matrix.

It is a swamp of bizarre electronic equipment. Vines of
coaxial hang and snake to and from huge monolithic battery
slabs, a black portable satellite dish and banks of life
systems and computer monitors.

At the center of the web, there are six ecto-skeleton chairs
made of a poly-alloy frame and suspension harness. Near the
circle of chairs is the control console and operator's
station where the network is monitored.

                        MORPHEUS
            You want to know what the Matrix
            is, Neo? The answer is right here.

He touches the back of Neo's head.

                        MORPHEUS
            Help him, Trinity.

Neo allows himself to be helped into one of the chairs. He
feels Morpheus guiding a coaxial line into the jack at the
back of his neck. The cable has the same kind of cerebrum
chip we saw inside the plant.

MORPHEUS
This will feel a little weird.

There are several disturbing noises as he works the needle in.

We move in as Neo's shoulders bunch and his face tightens into a grimace until a loud click fires and his ears pop like when you equalize them underwater.

He relaxes, opening his eyes as we pull back to a feeling of weightlessness inside another place--

39   **INT. CONSTRUCT**   39

Neo is standing in an empty, blank-white space.

MORPHEUS
This is the Construct.

Startled, Neo whips around and finds Morpheus now in the room with him.

MORPHEUS
It is our loading program. We can load anything from clothes, to weapons, to training simulations. Anything we need.

Morpheus walks past Neo and when Neo turns he sees the two leather chairs from the Hotel Lafayette set up in front of a large-screen television.

MORPHEUS
Sit down.

Neo stands at the back of the chair as Morpheus sits.

NEO
Right now, we're inside a computer program?

Morpheus smiles.

MORPHEUS
Is it so hard to believe? Your clothes are different, the plugs in your arms and head are gone. Look at your hair, you were bald a moment ago.

Neo touches his head.

                    MORPHEUS
          It's what we call residual self
          image. The mental projection of
          your electronic self. Wild, isn't
          it?

Neo's hands run over the cracked leather.

                    NEO
          This-- This isn't real?

                    MORPHEUS
          What is real? How do you define
          real? If you're talking about what
          you feel, taste, smell, or see,
          then real is simply electrical signals
          interpreted by your brain.

He picks up a remote control and clicks on the television. On
the television, we see images of the twentieth-century city
where Neo lived.

                    MORPHEUS
          This is the world you know. The
          world as it was at the end of the
          twentieth century. It exists now
          only as part of a neural-
          interactive simulation that we
          call the Matrix.

He changes the channel and we see a very different city as we
enter the television.

                    MORPHEUS
          You have been living inside a
          dreamworld, Neo. As in
          Baudrillard's vision, your whole
          life has been spent inside the
          map, not the territory. This is
          the world as it exists today.

In the distance, we see the ruins of a future city protruding
from the wasteland like the blackened ribs of a long-dead
corpse.

                    MORPHEUS
          'The desert of the real.'

Beneath us, the water is gone.

We turn and descend, spiraling down toward the lake bed which
is scorched and split like burnt flesh, where we find
Morpheus and Neo. Neo clings to the chair, trying to get his
bearings.

                  MORPHEUS
            We have only bits and pieces of
            information. What we know for
            certain is that, at some point in
            the early twenty-first century,
            all of mankind was united in
            celebration. Through the blinding
            inebriation of hubris, we marveled
            at our magnificence as we gave
            birth to A.I.

                  NEO
            A.I.? You mean artificial
            intelligence?

                  MORPHEUS
            Yes. A singular consciousness that
            spawned an entire race of
            machines. I must say I find it
            almost funny to imagine the world
            slapping itself on the back,
            toasting the new age. I say almost
            funny.

He looks up and his sunglasses reflect the obsidian clouds
roiling overhead.

                  MORPHEUS
            We don't know who struck first. Us
            or them. But we do know it was us
            that scorched the sky. At the
            time, they were dependent on solar
            power. It was believed they would
            be unable to survive without an
            energy source as abundant as the
            sun.

As we descend into the circular window of his glasses, there
is a flash of lightning.

                  MORPHEUS
            Throughout human history, we have
            been dependent on machines to
            survive. Fate, it seems, is not
            without a sense of irony.

40   EXT. FETUS FIELDS   **40**

On the flash, we pull back from the darkness which reveals
itself to be the black eye of a fetus.

                        MORPHEUS
            The Machines discovered a new form
            of fusion. All they needed was a
            small electrical charge to
            initiate the reaction.

The fetus is suspended in a placenta-like husk, where its
malleable skull is already growing around the brain-jack.

                        MORPHEUS
            The human body generates more
            bioelectricity than a 120-volt
            battery and over 25,000 B.T.U.'s
            of body heat.

The husk hanging from a stalk is plucked by a thresher-like
farm machine.

                        MORPHEUS
            There are fields, endless fields
            where human beings are no longer
            born; we are grown.

We rise up, the field stretching in every direction to the
horizon, lightning tearing open the sky as a harvester sweeps
past us.

A40   INT. POWER PLANT   A40

From the yawning black of the waste port, we begin to pull
back as it snaps shut.

Red amniotic gel flows into the pod below us, pooling around
a tiny newborn that suckles its feed tube.

                        MORPHEUS
            For the longest time, I wouldn't
            believe it. But then I saw the
            fields with my own eyes, watched
            them liquify the dead so they
            could be fed intravenously to the
            living and standing there, facing
            the efficiency, the pure,
            horrifying precision, I came to
            realize the obviousness of the
            truth.

Still pulling back, we see the image of the power plant now
on the television as we return to the white space of the
construct.

41   INT. CONSTRUCT   41

Morpheus steps into view as he clicks off the television.

40

                    MORPHEUS
          What is the Matrix? Control.

He opens the back of the television remote control.

                    MORPHEUS
          The Matrix is a computer-generated
          dreamworld built to keep us under
          control in order to change a human
          being into this.

He holds up a coppertop battery.

                    NEO
          No! I don't believe it! It's not
          possible!

                    MORPHEUS
          I didn't say that it would be
          easy, Neo. I just said that it
          would be the truth.

                    NEO
          Stop! Let me out! I want out!

42   **INT. MAIN DECK**   42

His eyes snap open and he thrashes against the chair, trying
to rip the cable from the back of his neck.

                    NEO
          Get this thing out of me!

                    TRINITY
          Easy, Neo. Easy.

Dozer holds him while Trinity unlocks it. Once it's out, he
tears away from them, falling as he trips free of the
harness.

                    NEO
          Don't touch me! Get away from me!

On his hands and knees, he reels as the world spins. Sweat
pours off him as a pressure builds inside his skull as if his
brain had been put into a centrifuge.

                    NEO
          I don't believe it! I don't
          believe it!

                    CYPHER
          He's going to pop!

Vomiting violently, Neo pitches forward and blacks out.

INT. NEO'S ROOM

He blinks, regaining consciousness. The room is dark. Neo is
stretched out on his bed.

                    NEO
          I can't go back, can I?

Morpheus is sitting like a shadow on a chair in the far
corner.

                    MORPHEUS
          No. But if you could, would you
          really want to?

Deep down, Neo knows that answer.

                    MORPHEUS
          I feel that I owe you an apology.
          There is a rule that we do not
          free a mind once it reaches a
          certain age. It is dangerous. They
          have trouble letting go. Their
          mind turns against them. I've seen
          it happen. I'm sorry. I broke the
          rule because I had to.

He stares into the darkness, confessing as much to himself as
to Neo.

                    MORPHEUS
          When the Matrix was first built
          there was a man born inside that
          had the ability to change what he
          wanted, to remake the Matrix as he
          saw fit. It was this man that
          freed the first of us and taught
          us the truth; as long as the
          Matrix exists, the human race will
          never be free.

He pauses.

                    MORPHEUS
          When he died, the Oracle
          prophesied his return and
          envisioned that his coming would
          hail the destruction of the
          Matrix, an end to the war and
          freedom for our people. That is
          why there are those of us that
          have spent our entire lives
          searching the Matrix, looking for
          him.

Neo can feel his eyes on him.

> MORPHEUS
> I did what I did because I believe
> the search is over.

He stands up.

> MORPHEUS
> Get some rest. You're going to
> need it.

> NEO
> For what?

> MORPHEUS
> Your training.

44   INT. HOVERCRAFT   44

There is no morning; there is only darkness and then the
fluorescent light sticks flicker on.

45   INT. NEO'S ROOM   45

Neo is awake in his bed, staring up at the lights. The door
opens and TANK steps inside.

> TANK
> Morning. Did you sleep?

> NEO
> No.

> TANK
> You will tonight. I guarantee it.
> I'm Tank. I'll be your operator.

He offers his hand and Neo shakes it. He notices that Tank
doesn't have any jacks.

> NEO
> You don't have...

> TANK
> Any holes? Nope. Me and my brother
> Dozer, we are 100 percent pure,
> old-fashioned, home-grown human.
> Born free. Right here in the real
> world. Genuine child of Zion.

> NEO
> Zion?

                    TANK
          If this war ended tomorrow, Zion
          is where the party would be.

                    NEO
          It's a city?

                    TANK
          The last human city. The only
          place we got left.

                    NEO
          Where is it?

                    TANK
          Deep underground. Near the earth's
          core, where it's still warm. You
          live long enough, you might even
          see it.

Tank smiles.

                    TANK
          Goddamn, I got to tell you, I'm
          fairly excited to see what you are
          capable of. I mean if Morpheus is
          right and all. We're not supposed
          to talk about any of that but if you
          are, well then this is an exciting
          time. We got a lot to do, so let's
          get to it.

46   INT. MAIN DECK   46

Neo is plugged in, hanging in one of the suspension chairs.

                    TANK
          We're supposed to load all these
          operations programs first, but
          this is some major boring shit.
          Why don't we start with something
          a little fun?

Tank smiles as he plops into his operator's chair. He begins
flipping through a tall carousel loaded with micro discs.

                    TANK
          How about some combat training?

Neo reads the label on the disk.

                    NEO
          Jujitsu? I'm going to learn
          jujitsu?

Tank slides the disk into Neo's supplement drive.

                    NEO
          No way.

Smiling, Tank punches the "load" code. His body jumps against
the harness as his eyes clamp shut. The monitors kick wildly
as his heart pounds, adrenaline surges, and his brain
sizzles. An instant later his eyes snap open.

                    NEO
          Holy shit!

                    TANK
          Hey, Mikey, he likes it! Ready for
          more?

                    NEO
          Hell yes!

47   **INT. MAIN DECK**   47

          Close on a computer monitor as grey pixels slowly fill a
          small, half-empty box. It is a meter displaying how much
          download time is left.

          The title bar reads: "Combat Series 10 of 12," file
          categories flashing beneath it: "Savate, Jujitsu, Ken Po,
          Drunken Boxing..."

          Morpheus walks in.

                    MORPHEUS
          How is he?

                    TANK
          Ten hours straight. He's a
          machine.

          Neo's body spasms and relaxes as his eyes open, breath
          hissing from his lips. He looks like he just orgasmed.

                    NEO
          This is incredible. I know kung
          fu.

                    MORPHEUS
          Show me.

They are standing in a very sparse Japanese-style dojo.

> MORPHEUS
> This is a sparring program,
> similar to the programmed reality
> of the Matrix. It has the same
> basic rules. Rules like gravity.
> What you must learn is that these
> rules are no different than the
> rules of a computer system. Some
> of them can be bent. Others can be
> broken. Understand?

Neo nods as Morpheus assumes a fighting stance.

> MORPHEUS
> Then hit me, if you can.

Neo assumes a similar stance, cautiously circling until he gives a short cry and launches a furious attack.

It is like a Jackie Chan movie at high speed, fists and feet striking from every angle as Neo presses his attack, but each and every blow is blocked by effortless speed.

49   INT. MAIN DECK   49

While their minds battle in the programmed reality, the two bodies appear quite serene, suspended in the drive chairs.

Tank monitors their Life Systems, noticing that Neo is wildly and chaotically lit up as opposed to the slow and steady rhythm of Morpheus.

50   INT. MESS HALL   50

MOUSE bursts into the room, interrupting dinner.

> MOUSE
> Morpheus is fighting Neo!

All at once, everyone bolts for the door.

51   INT. DOJO   51

Neo's face is knotted, teeth clenched, as he hurls himself at Morpheus.

> MORPHEUS
> Good. Adaptation. Improvisation. But
> your weakness isn't your technique.

Morpheus attacks him and it is like nothing we have seen. His feet and fists are everywhere, taking Neo apart. For every blow Neo blocks, five more hit their marks until--

Neo falls.

Panting, on his hands and knees, blood spits from his mouth, speckling the white floor of the dojo.

                    MORPHEUS
          How did I beat you?

                    NEO
          You-- you're too fast.

                    MORPHEUS
          Do you think my being faster,
          stronger has anything to do with
          my muscles in this place?

Neo is frustrated, still unable to catch his breath.

                    MORPHEUS
          Do you believe that's air you are
          breathing now?

Neo stands, nodding slowly.

                    MORPHEUS
          Again.

Their fists fly with pneumatic speed.

52   **INT. MAIN DECK**   52

Everyone is gathered behind Tank watching the fight, like watching a game of Mortal Kombat.

                    MOUSE
          Jeeezus Keeerist! He's fast! Look
          at his neural-kinetics! They're
          way above normal!

53   **INT. DOJO**   53

Morpheus begins to press Neo, countering blows while slipping in several stinging slaps.

                    MORPHEUS
          Come on, Neo. What are you waiting
          for? You're faster than this.
          Don't think you are. Know you are.

Whack, Morpheus cracks Neo again. Neo's face twists with rage as the speed of the blows rises like a drum solo.

47

MORPHEUS
Come on! Stop trying to hit me and
just hit me.

Wham. A single blow catches Morpheus on the side of the head,
knocking off his glasses.

54   **INT. MAIN DECK**   54

There are several gasps.

MOUSE
I don't believe it!

55   **INT. DOJO**   55

Morpheus rubs his face, then smiles.

NEO
I know what you're trying to do--

MORPHEUS
I'm trying to free your mind, Neo,
but all I can do is show you the
door. You're the one that has to
step through. Tank, load the jump
program.

56   **INT. HOVERCRAFT**   56

Apoc and Switch exchange looks as Tank grabs for the disk.

57   **INT. CONSTRUCT - ROOFTOP - DAY**   57

Morpheus and Neo are again in the white space of the
Construct. Beneath their feet, we see the jump program rush
up at them until they are standing on a rooftop in a city
skyline.

MORPHEUS
Let it all go, Neo. Fear. Doubt.
Disbelief. Free your mind.

Morpheus spins, running hard at the edge of the rooftop. And
jumps. He sails through the air, his coat billowing out
behind him like a cape as he lands on the rooftop across the
street.

NEO
Shit.

Neo looks down at the street twenty floors below, then at
Morpheus an impossible fifty feet away.

                              NEO
                    Okie dokie. Free my mind. Right.
                    No problem.

He takes a deep breath. And starts to run.

58   **INT. MAIN DECK**   58

They are transfixed.

                              MOUSE
                    What if he makes it?

                              APOC
                    No way. Not possible.

                              TANK
                    No one's ever made their first
                    jump.

                              MOUSE
                    I know but what if he does?

                              APOC
                    He won't.

Trinity stares at the screen, her fists clenching as she
whispers.

                              TRINITY
                    Come on.

59   **EXT. ROOFTOP**   59

Summoning every ounce of strength in his legs, Neo launches
himself into the air in a single maniacal shriek--

But comes up drastically short.

His eyes widen as he plummets. Stories fly by, the ground
rushing up at him, but as he hits, the ground gives way,
stretching like a trapeze net. He bounces and flips, slowly
coming to a rest, flat on his back.

He laughs, a bit unsure, wiping the wind-blown tears from his
face. Morpheus exits the building and helps him to his feet.

                              MORPHEUS
                    Do you know why you didn't make
                    it?

                              NEO
                    Because... I didn't think I would?

Morpheus smiles and nods.

60   INT. MAIN DECK   60

They break up.

                        MOUSE
                  What does it mean?

                        SWITCH
                  It doesn't mean anything.

                        CYPHER
                  Everyone falls the first time,
                  right, Trinity?

But Trinity has already left.

Neo's eyes open as Tank eases the plug out. He tries to move
and groans, cradling his ribs. While Tank helps Morpheus, Neo
spits blood into his hand.

                        NEO
                  I thought it wasn't real.

                        MORPHEUS
                  Your mind makes it real.

Neo stares at the blood.

                        NEO
                  If you are killed in the Matrix,
                  you die here?

                        MORPHEUS
                  The body cannot live without the
                  mind.

61   INT. NEO'S ROOM   61

Trinity enters from the hall, carrying a tray of food.

                        TRINITY
                  Neo, I saved you some dinner--

She sees him passed out on the bed. She sets the tray down
and pulls the blanket over him.

She pauses, her face close to his, then inhales lightly,
breathing in the scent of him before slowly pulling away.

62   INT. HALL   62

Trinity steps out of Neo's room to find Cypher watching her.

                    CYPHER
          I don't remember you ever bringing
          me dinner.

Trinity says nothing.

                    CYPHER
          There's something about him, isn't
          there?

                    TRINITY
          Don't tell me you're a believer
          now?

                    CYPHER
          I just keep wondering if Morpheus
          is so sure, why doesn't he take
          him to the Oracle? She would know.

                    TRINITY
          Morpheus will take him when he's
          ready.

She turns and he watches her walk away.

63   **EXT. CITY STREET - TRAINING PROGRAM - DAY**   63

Morpheus moves effortlessly through a crowded downtown street
while Neo struggles to keep up, constantly bumped and
shouldered off the path.

                    MORPHEUS
          The Matrix is a system, Neo, and
          that system is our enemy. But when
          you are inside and look around,
          what do you see; businessmen,
          lawyers, teachers, carpenters. The
          minds of the very people we are
          trying to save. But until we do,
          these people are still a part of
          the system and that makes them our
          enemy.

A cop writing a parking ticket stares at Neo from behind his
glasses.

                    MORPHEUS
          You have to understand that most
          of these people are not ready to
          be unplugged and many of them are
          so inured, so hopelessly dependent
          on the system that they will fight
          to protect it.

A beautiful woman in a red dress smiles at Neo as she passes
by.

                    MORPHEUS
               Were you listening to me, Neo? Or
               were you looking at the woman in
               the red dress?

                    NEO
               I was...

                    MORPHEUS
               Look again.

Neo turns just as Agent Smith levels a gun at his face. Neo
screams.

                    MORPHEUS
               Freeze it.

Everything except Morpheus and Neo freezes.

                    NEO
               This-- This isn't the Matrix?

                    MORPHEUS
               No, it's another training program
               designed to teach you one thing;
               if you are not one of us, you're
               one of them.

                    NEO
               What are they?

                    MORPHEUS
               Sentient programs. They can move
               in and out of any software still
               hardwired to their system. That
               means that anyone that we haven't
               unplugged is potentially an Agent.
               Inside the Matrix, they are
               everyone and they are no one.

Neo stares at the Agent.

                    MORPHEUS
               We've survived by hiding from
               them, running from them, but they
               are the gatekeepers, they're
               guarding all the doors, holding
               all the keys which means that
               sooner or later someone is going
               to have to fight them.

                    NEO
          Someone?

                    MORPHEUS
          I won't lie to you, Neo. Every
          single man or woman who has stood
          their ground, who has fought an
          Agent, has died. But where they
          failed, you will succeed.

                    NEO
          Why?

                    MORPHEUS
          I've seen an Agent punch through a
          concrete wall. Men have emptied
          entire clips at them and hit
          nothing but air. Yet their strength
          and their speed are still based in a
          world that is built by rules. Because
          of that, they will never be as strong
          or as fast as you can be.

Neo scratches his head.

                    NEO
          What? Are you trying to tell me
          that I can dodge bullets?

                    MORPHEUS
          No, Neo. I'm trying to tell you
          that when you're ready, you won't
          have to.

Morpheus's cell phone rings and he flips it open.

                    TANK (V.O.)
          We got trouble.

64   **EXT. SEWER MAIN**   64

The Nebuchadnezzar blisters by, trailing a swirling,
supercharged, electromagnetic wake.

65   **INT. COCKPIT**   65

Morpheus slides into the co-pilot's chair next to Dozer.

                    MORPHEUS
          Did Zion send the warning?

                    DOZER
          No. Another ship. Big Brother I
          think, they're running a parallel
          pipeline.

Morpheus scans the decayed landscape of the sewer main that
rolls by as Neo and Trinity squeeze into the cockpit behind
him. An alarm begins to sound.

                    DOZER
          Shit, Squiddy's sweeping in quick.

                    MORPHEUS
          Set it down in there.

                    NEO
          Squiddy?

                    TRINITY
          A Sentinel. It's a killing machine
          designed for one thing.

                    DOZER
          Search and destroy.

Neo feels the ship rock to the side as it squeezes into a
tiny supply line.

66   **EXT. HOVERCRAFT**   66

The Nebuchadnezzar sets down, almost wedged into a pipe that
barely accommodates its size.

67   **INT. COCKPIT**   67

Morpheus clicks the intercom.

                    MORPHEUS
          How we doing, Tank?

68   **INT. MAIN DECK**   68

Tank works furiously at the operator's station as the
ceaseless whir of the ship's turbines grind to a halt. The
main deck is plunged into dark silence. The rest of the crew
stands behind him as he whispers.

                    TANK
          Power off-line. E.M.P. armed and
          ready.

Tank's fingers curl around a small key that glows a dim red.

69   INT. COCKPIT   69

Neo leans into Trinity's ear.

                         NEO
            E.M.P?

                         TRINITY
            An electromagnetic pulse. It
            disables any electrical system in
            the blast radius. It's the only
            weapon we have against the
            machines.

Dozer looks up.

                         DOZER
            Now we wait.

Through the cockpit's windshield, the vast cavern of the
sewer main yawns before them. Strands of green haze curl
around mossy icicles that dangle into a pool of churning
frozen waste.

Neo begins to angle around Dozer but Morpheus grabs him.

                         MORPHEUS
            Don't move. It'll hear you.

Neo freezes and they wait. Without the Nebuchadnezzar's
heating systems, the temperature in the cockpit begins to
rapidly drop. The crew members huddle together, their breath
freezing into a uniform cloud as it gets colder and colder.

Dozer quietly reaches to brush away the frost on the
windshield and as his hand clears a swathe--

They see it.

In the darkness, a shifting shadow of mechanized death. It is
beautiful and terrifying. Black alloy skin flickers like
sequins beneath sinewy coils and skeletal appendages.

Neo can feel the hairs on the back of his neck rise as it
silently glides over them with shark-like malevolence until
it disappears into the darkness.

In the frozen little room, everyone breathes a little easier.

70   INT. HALL   70

The ship is quiet and dark. Everyone is asleep.

The core glows with monitor light. Cypher is in the
operator's chair as Neo comes up behind him.

                    CYPHER
          Whoa! Shit, Neo, you scared the
          Bejeezus out of me.

                    NEO
          Sorry.

                    CYPHER
          No, it's all right.

Neo's eyes light up as he steps closer to the screens that
seem alive with a constant flow of data.

                    NEO
          Is that...?

                    CYPHER
          The Matrix? Yeah.

Neo stares at the endlessly shifting river of information,
bizarre codes and equations flowing across the face of the
monitor.

                    NEO
          Do you always look at it encoded?

                    CYPHER
          Have to. The image translators
          sort of work for the construct
          programs but there's way too much
          information to decode the Matrix.
          You get used to it, though. Your
          brain does the translating. I
          don't even see the code. All I see
          is blonde, brunette, and redhead.
          You want a drink?

Neo nods and he pours a clear alcohol from a plastic jug.

                    CYPHER
          You know, I know what you're
          thinking 'cause right now I'm
          thinking the same thing. Actually,
          to tell you the truth, I've been
          thinking the same thing ever since
          I got here.

He raises the glass.

                    CYPHER
          Why, oh why, didn't I take that
          blue pill!?

He throws the shot down his throat. Neo does the same and it
almost kills him. Smiling, Cypher slaps him on the back.

                    CYPHER
          Good shit, eh? Dozer makes it.
          It's good for two things:
          degreasing engines and killing
          brain cells.

Red-faced, Neo finally stops coughing. Cypher pours him
another.

                    CYPHER
          Can I ask you something? Did he
          happen to tell you why he did it?

Neo looks up, unsure.

                    CYPHER
          Why you're here?

                    NEO
          ...yeah.

                    CYPHER
          Gee-zus! What a mindjob. You're
          here to save the world. You gotta
          be shitting me. What do you say to
          something like that?

Neo looks down at his drink.

                    CYPHER
          I'm going to let you in on a
          little secret here. Now don't tell
          him I told you this, but this
          ain't the first time Morpheus
          thought he found the One.

                    NEO
          Really?

                    CYPHER
          You bet your ass. It keeps him
          going. Maybe it keeps all of us
          going.

                    NEO
          How many were there?

                              CYPHER
                    Five. Since I've been here.

                              NEO
                    What happened to them?

                              CYPHER
                    Dead. All dead.

                              NEO
                    How?

                              CYPHER
                    Honestly? Morpheus. He got them
                    all amped up believing in bullshit.
                    I watched each of them take on an
                    Agent and I watched each of them die.
                    Little piece of advice: you see an
                    Agent, you do what we do; run. Run
                    your ass off.

          Neo gulps down another shot.

                              NEO
                    Thanks... for the drink.

                              CYPHER
                    Any time.

          Cypher nods as Neo heads for the ladder.

                              CYPHER
                    Sweet dreams.

A71   INT. RESTAURANT - NIGHT   A71

          Chamber music and the ambiance of wealth soak the restaurant
          around us as we watch a serrated knife saw through a thick,
          gorgeous steak. The meat is so perfect, charred on the
          outside, oozing red juice on the inside, that it could be a
          dream.

          We hear a voice that we recognize immediately.

                              AGENT SMITH
                    Do we have a deal, Mr. Reagan?

          A fork stabs the cube of meat and we follow it up to the face
          of Cypher.

58

                    CYPHER
          You know, I know that this steak
          doesn't exist. I know that when I
          put it in my mouth, the Matrix is
          telling my brain that it is juicy
          and delicious. After nine years,
          do you know what I've realized?

He shoves it in, eyes rolling up, savoring the tender beef
melting in his mouth.

                    CYPHER
          Ignorance is bliss.

Agent Smith watches him chew the steak loudly, smacking it
between his teeth.

                    CYPHER
          Mmm so, so goddamn good.

                    AGENT SMITH
          Then we have a deal?

                    CYPHER
          I don't want to remember nothing.
          Nothing! You understand? And I
          want to be rich. Someone
          important. Like an actor. You can
          do that, right?

                    AGENT SMITH
          Whatever you want, Mr. Reagan.

Cypher takes a deep drink of wine.

                    CYPHER
          All right. You get my body back in
          a Power Plant, reinsert me into
          the Matrix, and I'll get you what
          you want.

                    AGENT SMITH
          Access codes to the Zion
          mainframe.

                    CYPHER
          I told you I don't know them. But
          I can give you the man who does.

                    AGENT SMITH
          Morpheus.

Close on breakfast, a substance with a consistency somewhere between yogurt and cellulite.

> TANK
> Here you go, buddy. Breakfast of champions.

Tank slides it in front of Neo and takes a seat with the other crew members enjoying breakfast.

> MOUSE
> If you close your eyes, it almost feels like you're eating runny eggs.

> APOC
> Or a bowl of snot.

> MOUSE
> But you know what it really reminds me of? Tastee Wheat. Did you ever eat Tastee Wheat?

> SWITCH
> No, but technically neither did you.

> MOUSE
> Exactly my point, because you have to wonder, how do the machines know what Tastee Wheat really tasted like? Maybe they got it wrong, maybe what I think Tastee Wheat tasted like actually tasted like oatmeal, or tuna fish. It makes you wonder about a lot of things. Take chicken for example. Maybe they couldn't figure out what to make chicken taste like which is why chicken tastes like everything. And maybe--

> APOC
> Shut up, Mouse.

Neo scoops up a spoonful.

> DOZER
> It's a single-celled protein combined with synthetic aminos, vitamins, and minerals. Everything your body needs. We grow it in a vat.

                    MOUSE
          Oh no, it doesn't have everything
          the body needs.

He sidles up to Neo.

                    MOUSE
          So I understand you've run through
          the Agent training program? You
          know, I wrote that program.

                    APOC
          Here it comes.

                    MOUSE
          So what did you think of her?

                    NEO
          Of who?

                    MOUSE
          The woman in the red dress. I
          designed her. She doesn't talk
          much but if you'd like to, you
          know, meet her, I could arrange a
          more personalized milieu.

                    SWITCH
          The digital pimp hard at work.

                    MOUSE
          Pay no attention to these
          hypocrites, Neo. To deny our
          impulses is to deny the very thing
          that makes us human.

Morpheus enters.

                    MORPHEUS
          I want everyone on twelve-hour
          standby. We're going in. I'm
          taking Neo to see her.

With that he turns and leaves.

                    NEO
          See who?

                    TANK
          The Oracle.

A72   INT. MAIN DECK   A72

Everyone is strapped into their chairs. Tank is at the
operator's station.

                              TANK
                    All right, everyone please observe
                    that the no smoking and fasten
                    seat belt signs have been turned
                    on. Sit back and enjoy your
                    flight.

He strikes the enter key and we rush clockwise over the
chairs, each body reacting as we cut--

B72   INT. HOTEL LAFAYETTE - ROOM 1313   B72

         Spinning counter clockwise around an old phone that rings
         inside the empty room until we spin full circle and find
         everyone now standing there.

         Morpheus answers the phone.

                              MORPHEUS
                    We're in.

73   EXT. HOTEL LAFAYETTE - DAY   73

         The door opens and for the first time since his release, Neo
         steps back into the Matrix. He squints at the sun which seems
         unnaturally bright. He is the only one without sunglasses.

         Apoc and Switch remain at the door as the others enter the
         alley.

                              MORPHEUS
                    We should be back in an hour.

         Cypher opens the driver's door of an old car. As Trinity,
         Morpheus, and Neo cross to the car, Cypher glances about
         quickly, then drops something inside a garbage can.

         It is a cellular phone and we see its blue display as the
         line connects.

74   INT. CAR   74

         Neo sits beside Trinity in the back. He cannot stop staring
         as the simple images of the urban street blur past his window
         like an endless stream of data rushing down a computer
         screen.

                              MORPHEUS
                    Almost unbelievable, isn't it?

         Neo nods as the car continues to wind through the crowded
         city.

                              NEO
                    God...

                    TRINITY
          What?

                    NEO
          I used to eat there... Really good
          noodles...

He is speaking in a whisper, almost as if talking to himself.

                    NEO
          I have these memories, from my
          entire life but... none of them
          really happened.

He turns to her.

                    NEO
          What does that mean?

                    TRINITY
          That the Matrix cannot tell you
          who you are.

                    NEO
          But an Oracle can.

                    TRINITY
          That's different.

                    NEO
          Obviously.

He turns to the window for a moment and then turns back.

                    NEO
          Did you go to her?

                    TRINITY
          Yes.

                    NEO
          What did she tell you?

                    TRINITY
          She told me...

She looks at him and suddenly she is unable to speak or even
breathe.

                    NEO
          What?

The car suddenly jerks to a stop.

                    MORPHEUS
             We're here. Neo, come with me.

Neo and Morpheus get out of the car. Cypher looks into the
rearview mirror at Trinity.

                    CYPHER
             Here we go again, eh, Trin?

He smiles as she turns to the window.

75   **EXT. BUILDING**   75

     Tenement-like and vast, it is the kind of place where people
     can disappear.

76   **INT. BUILDING**   76

     Morpheus nods to a blind man who nods back. An elevator opens
     and Neo follows Morpheus inside.

77   **INT. ELEVATOR**   77

     The idea of learning one's fate begins to weigh upon Neo with
     a steadily growing unease.

                    NEO
             So is this the same oracle that
             made the, uh, prophecy?

                    MORPHEUS
             Yes. She's very old. She's been
             with us since the beginning.

                    NEO
             The beginning?

                    MORPHEUS
             Of the Resistance.

                    NEO
             And she knows what? Everything?

                    MORPHEUS
             She would say she knows enough.

                    NEO
             And she's never wrong.

                    MORPHEUS
             Don't think of it in terms of
             right and wrong. She is a guide,
             Neo. She can help you find the
             path.

                    NEO
              She helped you?

                    MORPHEUS
              Yes.

                    NEO
              What did she tell you?

                    MORPHEUS
              That I would find the One.

Ding. The elevator opens.

78   INT. HALL   **78**

The long dark hall beckons. Neo follows Morpheus out of the
elevator and the doors rattle shut behind him. With every
step, a disturbing sense of inevitability closes in around
him.

At the end of the hall, Morpheus steps to the side of a door.

                    MORPHEUS
              I told you that I can only show
              you the door. You have to step
              through it.

Neo blows out a breath. His hand reaches but stops, hovering
over the spherical handle. He backs away.

                    NEO
              Morpheus, I don't think this is a
              good idea.

                    MORPHEUS
              Why?

                    NEO
              I told you I don't believe in this
              stuff. No matter what she says I'm
              not going to believe it, so what's
              the point?

                    MORPHEUS
              What do you believe in?

                    NEO
              What do I believe in? Are you
              kidding me? What do you think? The
              world I grew up in, isn't real. My
              entire life was a lie. I don't
              believe in anything anymore.

                    MORPHEUS
            That's why we're here.

                    NEO
            Why? So I can hear some old lady
            tell me, what? That I'm this guy
            that everybody's been waiting for?
            That I'm supposed to save the
            world? It sounds insane.
            Unbelievable. And I don't care who
            says it, it's still going to sound
            insane and unbelievable.

                    MORPHEUS
            Faith is not a matter of
            reasonability. I do not believe
            things with my mind. I believe
            them with my heart. In my gut.

                    NEO
            And you believe I'm the One?

                    MORPHEUS
            Yes I do.

                    NEO
            Yeah? What about the other five
            guys? The five before me? What
            about them?

Morpheus tries to hide his heart being wrenched from his
chest.

                    NEO
            Did you believe in them too?

                    MORPHEUS
            I believed what the Oracle told
            me.... No, I misunderstood what she
            told me. I believed that it was
            all about me.

This is difficult for Morpheus to admit.

                    MORPHEUS
            I believed that all I had to do
            was point my finger and anoint
            whoever I chose. I was wrong, Neo.
            Terribly wrong. Not a day or night
            passes that I do not think of
            them. After the fifth, I lost my
            way. I doubted everything the
            Oracle had said. I doubted myself.

He looks up at Neo.

                    MORPHEUS
          And then I saw you, Neo, and my
          world changed. You can call it an
          epiphany, you can call it whatever
          the hell you want. It doesn't
          matter. It's not about a word.
          It's about this. So I can't
          explain it to you. All I can do is
          believe, Neo, believe that one day
          you will feel what I felt and know
          what I know; you are the sixth and
          the last. You are the One.

His eyes blaze.

                    MORPHEUS
          Until that time all I am asking
          from you is for you to hold on to
          whatever respect you may have for
          me and trust me.

Neo feels a rush from Morpheus's intensity, the unadulterated
confidence of a zealot.

                    NEO
          All right.

He reaches for the handle which turns without him even
touching it. A WOMAN wearing white opens the door.

                    PRIESTESS (WOMAN)
          Hello, Neo. You're right on time.

79   INT. ORACLE'S APARTMENT   79

It seems particularly normal.

                    PRIESTESS
          Make yourself at home, Morpheus.

                    MORPHEUS
          Thank you.

                    PRIESTESS
          Neo, come with me.

She leads Neo down another hall and into what appears to be a
family room.

There is another woman in white sitting on a couch watching a
soap opera. Scattered about the room are a half dozen
children. Some of them are playing, others are deep in
meditation. All of them exude a kind of Zen calm.

                    PRIESTESS
          These are the other Potentials.
          You can wait here.

Neo watches a little girl levitate wooden alphabet blocks.
Closer to him, a SKINNY BOY with a shaved head holds a spoon
which sways like a blade of grass.

In front of him is a pile of spoons bent and twisted into
knots. Neo crosses to him and sits. The boy smiles and hands
Neo the spoon which is now perfectly straight.

                    SPOON BOY
          Do not try to bend the spoon. That
          is impossible. Instead, only try
          to realize the truth.

                    NEO
          What truth?

                    SPOON BOY
          That there is no spoon.

Neo nods, staring at the spoon.

                    NEO
          There is no spoon.

                    SPOON BOY
          Then you will see that it is not
          the spoon that bends. It is only
          yourself.

The entire room is reflected inside the spoon and as Neo
stares into it, it slowly begins to bend until--

A hand touches his shoulder.

                    PRIESTESS
          The Oracle will see you now.

Spoon Boy smiles.

80   INT. KITCHEN   80

An OLD WOMAN is huddled beside the oven, peering inside
through a cracked door.

                    NEO
          Hello?

                    ORACLE (OLD WOMAN)
          I know. You're Neo. Be right with
          you.

                    NEO
          You're the Oracle?

                    ORACLE
          Bingo. Not quite what you were
          expecting, right? I got to say I
          love seeing you non-believers.
          Always a pip. Almost done. Smell
          good, don't they?

                    NEO
          Yeah.

                    ORACLE
          I'd ask you to sit down, but
          you're not going to anyway. And
          don't worry about the vase.

                    NEO
          What vase?

He turns to look around and his elbow knocks a vase from the
table. It breaks against the linoleum floor.

                    ORACLE
          That vase.

                    NEO
          Shit, I'm sorry.

She pulls out a tray of chocolate chip cookies and turns. She
is an older woman, wearing big oven mitts, comfortable slacks,
and a print blouse. She looks like someone's grandma.

                    ORACLE
          I said don't worry about it. I'll
          get one of my kids to fix it.

                    NEO
          How did you know...?

She sets the cookie tray on a wooden hot pad.

                    ORACLE
          What's really going to bake your
          noodle later on is, would you
          still have broken it if I hadn't
          said anything.

Smiling, she lights a cigarette.

                    ORACLE
          You're cuter than I thought. I see
          why she likes you.

                    NEO
          Who?

                    ORACLE
          Not too bright though.

She winks.

                    ORACLE
          You know why Morpheus brought you
          to see me?

He nods.

                    ORACLE
          So? What do you think? You think
          you're the One?

                    NEO
          Honestly? I don't know.

She gestures to a wooden plaque, the kind every kitchen has,
except that the words are in Latin.

                    ORACLE
          You know what that means?
          It's Latin. Means, "Know Thyself."
          I'm gonna let you in on a little
          secret. Being the One is just
          like being in love. Nobody can
          tell you you're in love. You just
          know it. Through and through. Balls
          to bones.

She puts her cigarette down.

                    ORACLE
          Well, I better have a look at you.
          Open your mouth. Say "Ahh."

She widens his eyes, checks his ears, then feels the glands
in his neck. She nods then looks at his palms.

                    ORACLE
          Okay, now I'm supposed to say,
          "Hmmm, that's interesting but..."
          Then you say--

                    NEO
          But what?

                    ORACLE
          But you already know what I'm
          going to tell you.

                    NEO
          I'm not the One.

                    ORACLE
          Sorry, kid. You got the gift but
          looks like you're waiting for
          something.

                    NEO
          What?

                    ORACLE
          Your next life, maybe. Who knows.
          That's how these things go.

Neo almost has to laugh.

                    ORACLE
          What's funny?

                    NEO
          Morpheus. He almost had me
          convinced.

                    ORACLE
          I know. Poor Morpheus. Without him
          we are lost.

                    NEO
          What do you mean, without him?

The Oracle takes a long drag, regarding Neo with the eyes of
a Sphinx.

                    ORACLE
          Are you sure you want to hear
          this?

Neo nods.

                    ORACLE
          Morpheus believes in you, Neo and
          no one, not you or even me can
          convince him otherwise. He
          believes it so blindly that he's
          going to sacrifice his life to
          save yours.

                    NEO
          What?

                    ORACLE
          You're going to have to make a
          choice. In one hand, you will have
          Morpheus's life. In the other
          hand, you will have your own. One
          of you is going to die. Which one,
          will be up to you.

Neo can't breathe.

                    ORACLE
          I'm sorry, kiddo. I really am. You
          have a good soul and I hate giving
          good people bad news. But don't
          worry, as soon as you walk outside
          that door, you'll start feeling
          better. You'll remember that you
          don't believe any of this fate
          crap. You're in control of your
          own life, remember?

He tries to nod as she reaches for the tray of cookies.

                    ORACLE
          Here, take a cookie. I promise by
          the time you're done eating it,
          you'll feel right as rain.

Neo takes a cookie, the tightness in his chest slowly
beginning to fade.

81   **INT. SITTING ROOM - DAY**   81

Morpheus rises from a couch as the Priestess escorts Neo out.
When they are alone, Morpheus puts his hand on Neo's
shoulder.

                    MORPHEUS
          You don't have to tell anyone what
          she told you. What was said was
          said for you and you alone.

Neo nods and takes a bite of his cookie.

82   **INT. CAR**   82

Neo and Morpheus get in the car.

                    MORPHEUS
          Let's go.

Cypher looks into the rearview mirror at Neo.

                          CYPHER
            Well, good news or bad news?

                         MORPHEUS
            Not now, Cypher.

Cypher slaps the car in gear and pulls into traffic. Trinity
looks at Neo who is staring at the final bit of cookie. He
puts it in his mouth and chews.

                         TRINITY
            Are you all right?

                           NEO
            ...right as rain.

83   **SCENE OMITTED**   83

84   **INT. ROOM 1313 - DAY**   84

Mouse's cellular rings.

                          MOUSE
            Welcome to Movie-Phone.

                       TANK (V.O.)
            They're on their way.

85   **EXT. CITY STREET - DAY**   85

As they get out of the car, Cypher smiles at Neo.

                         CYPHER
            Like the man says, welcome to the
            real world.

Cypher, following the others into the hotel, nervously
glances around, wiping the sweat from his forehead.

86   **INT. MAIN DECK**   86

Sweat rolls down Cypher's face and neck. At the operator's
station, Tank is typing rapidly.

                          TANK
            What is that...?

87   **INT. HOTEL LAFAYETTE - DAY**   87

Light filters down the throat of the building, through a
caged skylight at the top of the open elevator shaft. Six
figures glide up the dark stairs that wind around the antique
elevator.

Neo notices a black cat, a yellow-green-eyed shadow that
slinks past them and pads quickly down the stairs.

A moment later, Neo sees another black cat that looks and
moves identically to the first one.

                    NEO
          Whoa. Deja vu.

Those words stop the others dead in their tracks.

88   INT. MAIN DECK   88

The monitors suddenly glitch as though the Matrix had an
electronic seizure.

                    TANK
          Oh shit! Oh shit!

89   INT. HOTEL LAFAYETTE - DAY   89

Trinity turns around, her face tight.

                    TRINITY
          What did you just say?

                    NEO
          Nothing. Just had a little deja
          vu.

                    TRINITY
          What happened? What did you see?

                    NEO
          A black cat went past us and then
          I saw another that looked just
          like it.

                    TRINITY
          How much like it? Was it the same
          cat?

                    NEO
          It might have been. I'm not sure.

Trinity looks at Morpheus who listens quietly to the rasping
breath of the old building.

                    NEO
          What is it?

                    TRINITY
          A deja vu is usually a glitch in
          the Matrix. It happens when they
          change something.

She also listens as the staccato beat of helicopter blades grows ominously loud.

90   **INT. MAIN DECK**   90

Tank sees what was changed.

                          TANK
                    It's a trap!

91   **INT. STAIRCASE - DAY**   91

Morpheus looks up the stairs as he hears a helicopter.

                        MORPHEUS
                    Come on!

Apoc slaps a gun in Neo's hand.

                          APOC
                    I hope the Oracle gave you some
                    good news.

Neo nods, stuffing it into his belt.

92   **INT. BASEMENT - DAY**   92

Heavy bolt cutters snap through the main phone cable.

93   **INT. ROOM 1313 - DAY**   93

Hearing the helicopter, Mouse goes to the draped windows as his cellular rings. He answers it.

                        TANK (V.O.)
                    They cut the hardline! It's a
                    trap! Get out!

Mouse yanks open the curtain.

                         MOUSE
                    Oh no.

The windows are bricked up. Mouse spins as the rumble of combat boots builds, then explodes into the room.

94   **INT. MAIN DECK**   94

Tank watches helplessly.

                          TANK
                    No, no, no.

95   INT. STAIRS - DAY   95

Morpheus stops as Mouse's scream is drowned out by the report
of machine gun fire.

96   INT. ROOM 1313 - DAY   96

Mouse sails backwards as bullets pound him against the blood-
spattered brick window.

97   INT. MAIN DECK   97

Mouse's body thrashes against its harness, blood coughing
from his mouth in one final spasm, then lying perfectly
still. The flatline alarm softly cries out from the life
monitor.

98   SCENE OMITTED   98

99   INT. STAIRWELL - DAY   99

Flying downstairs, Morpheus stops, hearing police swarming
below.

A99   INT. HALL - DAY   A99

He turns and rushes down the hall of the eighth floor. At the
end of it, he finds the bricked-up windows.

                    CYPHER
              That's what they changed. We're
              trapped. There's no way out.

The sound of heavy bootsteps close around them with the
mechanical sureness of a vice.

                    MORPHEUS
              Give me your phone.

                    TRINITY
              They'll be able to track it.

                    MORPHEUS
              We have no choice.

Morpheus rips off his jacket.

100   INT. MAIN DECK   100

Tank answers the call.

                    MORPHEUS (V.O.)
              Tank, find a structural drawing of
              this building and find it fast.

101   **INT. HOTEL LAFAYETTE - DAY**   101

Flashlights probe the rotting darkness as the police search
every floor.

102   **INT. MAIN DECK**   102

The diagram windows onto the screen.

                    TANK
            Got it.

                    MORPHEUS (V.O.)
            I need the main wet-wall.

103   **INT. ROOM 1313 - DAY**   103

Agent Smith stands over Mouse's dead body, his hand going to
his earpiece.

104   **INT. ROOM 808 - DAY**   104

Morpheus is guided by Tank.

                    TANK (V.O.)
            Now left and that's it in front of
            you.

                    MORPHEUS
            Good.

105   **INT. ROOM 1313 - DAY**   105

Agent Smith hears the line click dead.

                    AGENT SMITH
            Eighth floor. They're on the
            eighth floor.

A105   **INT. STAIRWELL - DAY**   A105

Agent Brown listens to his ear-piece.

106   **INT. STAIRWELL - DAY**   106

Boots clatter up the marble staircase.

A106   **INT. HALL - DAY**   A106

Cops flood the eighth floor, rushing everywhere.

107   **INT. ROOM 808 - DAY**   107

Several cops sweep through the room. It is empty. As they
pass the bathroom, we see a man-sized hole smashed through
the plaster and lath.

                                                               77

108   INT. WALL - DAY   108

They are inside the main plumbing wall, slowly worming their
way down the grease black stack pipes. Above them, light
fills the hole they made to get inside.

109   INT. HALL - DAY   109

Agent Brown and Agent Smith stand over Morpheus's jacket.

                    AGENT BROWN
              Where are they?

110   INT. ROOM 608 - DAY   110

The cops search in silence, straining for a clue, when one
hears something strange near the bathroom.

111   INT. WALL - DAY   111

Cypher has slipped and is wedged between the wall and several
thick supply pipes.

112   INT. ROOM 608 - DAY   112

The cop leans in, his ear almost against the thin membrane of
plaster separating them. He can hear whispers, hisses, and a
grunt when--

The wall suddenly bulges, shatter-cracking as the Cop
realizes--

                    COP
              They're in the walls!

113   INT. WALL - DAY   113

Trinity pulls Cypher free just as the Cop opens fire, bullets
punching shafts of light like swords into the box of soot-
black space.

Neo finds his gun first and begins blasting blindly through
the plaster and lath.

114   INT. ROOM 608 - DAY   114

The Cop spins out of the bathroom for cover, Neo's bullets
splintering the door jamb.

About to whirl back in, he freezes as something seems to
seize hold of him. The Cop's body starts to spasm and his
M-16 falls to the ground, long shadows springing up from the
mounted flashlight.

Neo listens for a moment, the gunfire quiet when he hears footsteps rising fast.

Two arms suddenly smash through the wall, punching Neo back against the iron stack pipe, fingers gouging into his neck.

> CYPHER
> It's an Agent!

Just as Neo's throat is about to collapse, Morpheus explodes through the tattered plaster and lath, diving on top of Agent Smith.

The two men crash to the wet terrazzo floor.

Before Agent Smith can find his weapon, Morpheus is on him, pinning him in an iron grip.

In the crawlspace, Trinity tries to scramble up past Cypher.

> TRINITY
> Morpheus!

Morpheus squeezes Agent Smith's throat.

> MORPHEUS
> Trinity, you must get Neo out. Do
> you understand? He is all that
> matters.

Neo suddenly glimpses what is happening but is powerless to stop it.

> NEO
> No. No! Morpheus! Don't!

> MORPHEUS
> Trinity! Go!

Trinity's fists ball in frustration. She yells down to Apoc.

> TRINITY
> Go!

> NEO
> We can't leave him!

> TRINITY
> We have to!

She grabs his ankle and they begin almost falling using the
lath as a brake, skidding down the inside of the wall.

116   INT. BASEMENT - DAY   116

This part of the basement, a dark concrete cavern, was the
main mechanical room. There are four enormous boilers,
dinosaur-like technology that once pumped hot water like
arteries.

Soldiers' blinding lights cut open the darkness as Trinity,
Neo, and the others crash through the ceiling. Around them
they hear a chorus of short, sharp coughs of grenade
launchers from gas-masked figures.

Smoke blossoms from the green metal canisters. Trinity never
stops moving. Searching the floor, she finds what she needs;
the cover of the catch basin.

Cypher watches her pry open the grate, when a gas can bounces
near him.

                    TRINITY
              Come on!

Cypher seems to trip as the cloud envelops him.

Trinity watches Cypher disappear into the smoke, then follows
the others down the wet-black hole.

117   INT. ROOM 608 - DAY   117

Morpheus and Agent Smith remain on the ground, locked in each
other's death grip.

                    AGENT SMITH
              The great Morpheus. We meet at
              last.

                    MORPHEUS
              And you are?

                    AGENT SMITH
              Smith. I am Agent Smith.

                    MORPHEUS
              You all look the same to me.

Agent Smith counters Morpheus and slowly begins to pry his
hands from his throat. Striking like a viper, Morpheus drives
a vicious head butt into Agent Smith's face. His nose and
glasses shatter.

Agent Smith, unfazed, smiles, blood oozing from the shattered
bridge of his nose and returns Morpheus's head butt with three
of his own in pneumatic succession.

Morpheus staggers back, his body going slack when another
kick buries him deep into crunching plaster and lath.

Morpheus turns in time to see a wall of men in the doorway.

                    AGENT SMITH
               Take him.

The wall of Cops rush Morpheus, filling the tiny bathroom
until he disappears under the tide.

118   **INT. MAIN DECK**   118

Tank reaches out to the screen as if reaching for Morpheus.

                    TANK
               No!

119   **SCENE OMITTED**   119

120   **EXT. STREET - DAY**   120

A manhole cover cracks open. Two eyes peek out just as a
truck rattles over it. The thunder dopplers away and the
cover opens. Trinity climbs out.

121   **INT. MAIN DECK**   121

Tank is again at the monitors, searching the Matrix when the
phone rings.

                    TANK
               Operator.

                    CYPHER (V.O.)
               I need an exit! Fast!

                    TANK
               Cypher?

122   **EXT. STREET - DAY**   122

Cypher is standing at a public phone. Across the street is
the burning paddy wagon that appears to have collided with an
oncoming car.

                    CYPHER
               There was an accident. A goddamn
               car accident. All of a sudden.
                    (MORE)

                         CYPHER   (cont'd)
          Boom. Jesus, someone up there
          still likes me.

                         TANK (V.O.)
          I got you.

                         CYPHER
          Just get me outta here.

                         TANK (V.O.)
          Nearest exit is Franklin and Erie.
          An old T.V. repair shop.

     Cypher hangs up and smiles as we hear fire trucks in the
     distance.

                         CYPHER
          An actor. Definitely.

123   **INT. MAIN DECK**   123

     The phone rings. Tank answers.

                         TRINITY (V.O.)
          Tank, it's me.

124   **EXT. STREET - DAY**   124

     All four are moving quickly down a back street.

                         NEO
          Is Morpheus alive?

                         TRINITY
          Is Morpheus still alive, Tank?

                         TANK (V.O.)
          Yes. They're moving him. I don't
          know where yet.

                         TRINITY
          He's alive.

     Again, inevitability seems to cinch around Neo.

                         TRINITY
          We need an exit!

                         TANK (V.O.)
          You're not far from Cypher.

                         TRINITY
          Cypher, I thought--

                         TANK (V.O.)
                    So did we. I sent him to Franklin
                    and Erie.

                         TRINITY
                    Got it.

A124   **EXT. T.V. REPAIR SHOP - DAY**   A124

        In a deserted alley, Cypher steps onto a dumpster in front of
        a small boarded-up window.

125   **INT. T.V. REPAIR SHOP - DAY**   125

        Dead machines, eviscerated and shrouded with dust, lay on
        metal shelves like bodies in a morgue. Plywood covering a
        window is ripped off and Cypher crawls inside.

        Deep in the back room, a phone that has not rung in years
        begins to ring.

126   **EXT. STREET - DAY**   126

        Trinity sees the T.V. repair shop.

127   **INT. MAIN DECK**   127

        Tank punches the exit command.

                         TANK
                    Got him.

        Cypher's body twitches in its harness, jerking itself awake.

128   **INT. T.V. REPAIR SHOP - DAY**   128

        Neo crawls through the window that Cypher opened.

129   **INT. MAIN DECK**   129

        Tank finishes loading the exit program as Cypher pulls back a
        heavy blanket, exposing a high-tech rifle.

130   **INT. T.V. REPAIR SHOP - DAY**   130

        The phone begins to ring as the others crawl in.

                         SWITCH
                    God, I love that sound.

131   **INT. MAIN DECK**   131

        Suddenly, a white bolt of lightning explodes against Tank's
        chair, blasting him into the air.

                                                                  83

Cypher checks the gun, unable to believe he missed.

                    CYPHER
          Shit.

Tank is on his feet, lunging when Cypher fires again, square
into his chest.

                    DOZER
              No!

132   INT. T.V. REPAIR SHOP - DAY   132

The phone is still ringing.

                    TRINITY
               You first, Neo.

Neo answers the phone when there is a click. There is no
signal. Nothing but silence.

                    TRINITY
               What happened?

                    NEO
               I don't know. It just went dead.

Trinity listens to the dead line and takes out the cellular.

133   INT. MAIN DECK   133

The operator phone begins to ring. Cypher steps over the
sizzling body of Dozer and looks at the monitor.

134   INT. T.V. REPAIR SHOP - DAY   134

Every unanswered ring wrings her gut a little tighter, until--

                    CYPHER (V.O.)
               Hello, Trinity.

                    TRINITY
               Cypher? Where's Tank?

                    CYPHER (V.O.)
               He had an accident.

                    TRINITY
               An accident?!

135   INT. MAIN DECK/T.V. REPAIR SHOP [INTERCUT]   135

He walks over to Trinity's body, staring down at it hanging
in its coma-like stillness.

84

                              CYPHER
                    You know, for a long time, I
                    thought I was in love with you,
                    Trinity. I used to dream about
                    you...

He nuzzles his face against hers, feeling the softness of it.

                              CYPHER
                    You are a beautiful woman. Too bad
                    things had to work out like this.

                              TRINITY
                    You killed them.

                              APOC
                    What?!

                              SWITCH
                    Oh, God.

Wearing Tank's operator headgear, Cypher moves among the
silent bodies.

                              CYPHER
                    I'm tired, Trinity. I'm tired of
                    this war, I'm tired of fighting.
                    I'm tired of this ship, of being
                    cold, of eating the same goddamn
                    goop every day. But most of all,
                    I'm tired of this jagoff and all
                    of his bullshit.

Cypher leans over, talking to Morpheus.

                              CYPHER
                    Surprise, asshole. Bet you never
                    saw this coming, did you? God, I
                    wish I could be there when they
                    break you. I wish I could walk in
                    just as it happens, so right then,
                    you'd know it was me.

                              TRINITY
                    My God. Morpheus. You gave them
                    Morpheus.

                              CYPHER
                    He lied to us, Trinity! He tricked
                    us! If he would've told us the
                    truth, we would've told him to
                    shove that red pill up his ass!

                              TRINITY
                    That's not true, Cypher. He set us
                    free.

                    CYPHER
          Free? You call this free? All I do
          is what he tells me to do. If I
          have to choose between that and
          the Matrix, I choose the Matrix.

                    TRINITY
          The Matrix isn't real!

                    CYPHER
          Oh, I disagree, Trinity. I
          disagree. I think the Matrix can
          be more real than this world. I
          mean, all I do is pull a plug
          here. But there, you have to watch
          Apoc die.

She looks up at Apoc, her face going white.

                    APOC
          Trinity?

He grabs hold of the cable in Apoc's neck, twists it, and
yanks it out.

                    CYPHER
          Welcome to the real world, eh
          baby?

Apoc seems to go blind for an instant, a scream caught in his
throat, his hands reaching for nothing, and then falls dead.

                    SWITCH
          No!

                    TRINITY
          But you're out, Cypher. You can't
          go back.

                    CYPHER
          That's what you think. They've
          promised to take me back. They're
          going to reinsert my body. I'll go
          back to sleep and when I wake up,
          I'll be fat and rich and I won't
          remember a goddamned thing. It's
          the American dream.

He laughs, his hand sliding around the neck of Switch as he
takes hold of her plug.

                    CYPHER
          By the way, if you have anything
          terribly important to say to
          Switch, I suggest you say it now.

                    TRINITY
          Oh no, please don't.

Trinity's eyes find Switch and she knows she's next.

                    SWITCH
          Not like this. Not like this.

She suddenly feels her body severed from her mind as she is
murdered.

                    CYPHER
          Too late.

                    TRINITY
          Goddamn you, Cypher!

                    CYPHER
          Don't hate me, Trinity. I'm just
          the messenger. And right now I'm
          going to prove it to you.

He stands over Neo.

                    CYPHER
          If Morpheus was right, then
          there's no way I can pull this
          plug, is there?

She turns to Neo, eyes wide with fear and he knows he is
next.

                    CYPHER
          If Neo is the One, then in the
          next few seconds there has to be
          some kind of miracle to stop me.
          Right? How can he be the One if
          he's dead?

He takes hold of the cord.

                    CYPHER
          You never did answer me, Trinity,
          when I asked you before. Did you
          buy Morpheus's bullshit? Come on.
          You can tell me, did you? All I
          want is a little yes or no. Look
          into his eyes, Trinity, those big
          pretty eyes and tell me the truth.
          Yes or no.

Trinity stares at Neo as a single word falls soundlessly from
her lips.

                    TRINITY
          ...yes.

                                                              87

                              CYPHER
                    No!

Charred and bloody, Tank levels the gun.

                              CYPHER
                    I don't believe it!

                              TANK
                    Believe it or not, you piece of
                    shit, you're still going to burn.

He fires a crackling bolt of lightning that knocks Cypher
flying backwards.

136   **SCENE OMITTED**   136

137   **INT. T.V. REPAIR SHOP - DAY**   137

           Trinity throws her arms around Neo and for a moment they are
           alone and alive until the phone rings.

                              NEO
                    Go. You first this time.

138   **INT. MAIN DECK**   138

           Trinity's eyes snap open, a sense of relief surging through
           her at the sight of the ship. As Tank unplugs her, she sees
           his charred wounds.

                              TRINITY
                    Tank, you're hurt.

                              TANK
                    I'll be all right.

                              TRINITY
                    Dozer?

           Tank's face tightens and she takes him into her arms.

139   **EXT. GOVERNMENT BUILDING - DAY**   139

           A government high-rise in the middle of downtown where a
           military helicopter sets down on the roof.

           Agent Jones gets out of the helicopter, flanked by columns of
           Marines. They open the roof access door and enter the top
           floor maintenance level of the building.

140   **INT. EXECUTIVE OFFICE - DAY**   140

           Agent Smith stands, staring out the windows at the city below
           shimmering with brilliant sunlight.

                    AGENT SMITH
          Have you ever stood and stared at
          it, Morpheus? Marveled at its
          beauty. Its genius. Billions of
          people just living out their
          lives... oblivious.

Morpheus is handcuffed to a chair, stripped to the waist. He
is alternately shivering and sweating, wired to various
monitors with white disk electrodes. Beside him, Agent Brown
sucks a serum from a glass vial, filling a hypodermic needle.

                    AGENT SMITH
          Did you know that the first Matrix
          was designed to be a perfect human
          world? Where none suffered, where
          everyone would be happy. It was a
          disaster. No one would accept the
          program. Entire crops were lost.

Agent Brown jams the needle into Morpheus's shoulder and
plunges down.

                    AGENT SMITH
          Some believed we lacked the
          programming language to describe
          your perfect world. But I believe
          that, as a species, human beings
          define their reality through
          suffering and misery.

Agent Brown studies the screens as the life signs react
violently to the injection.

                    AGENT SMITH
          The perfect world was a dream that
          your primitive cerebrum kept
          trying to wake up from. Which is
          why the Matrix was redesigned to
          this: the peak of your civilization.

He turns from the window.

                    AGENT SMITH
          I say 'your civilization' because as
          soon as we started thinking for you,
          it really became our civilization,
          which is, of course, what this is
          all about.

He sits down directly in front of Morpheus.

                    AGENT SMITH
              Evolution, Morpheus. Evolution.

He lifts Morpheus's head.

                    AGENT SMITH
              Like the dinosaur. Look out that
              window. You had your time.

Morpheus stares hard at him, trying not to show the pain
racking his mind.

                    AGENT SMITH
              The future is our world, Morpheus.
              The future is our time.

Agent Smith looks at Agent Brown.

                    AGENT SMITH
              Double the dosage.

Agent Jones suddenly enters.

                    AGENT JONES
              There could be a problem.

141   INT. MAIN DECK   **141**

Tank drapes a sheet over his dead brother. The other bodies are
covered.

Neo looks at Morpheus whose body is covered with a cold sweat.

                    NEO
              What are they doing to him?

                    TANK
              They're breaking into his mind.
              It's like hacking a computer. All
              it takes is time.

                    NEO
              How much time?

                    TANK
              Depends on the mind. But eventually,
              it will crack and his alpha pattern
              will change from this to this.

Tank punches several commands on Morpheus's personal unit.
The monitor waves change from a chaotic pattern to an ordered
symmetrical one.

                    TANK
          When it does, Morpheus will tell
          them anything they want to know.

                    NEO
          What do they want?

                    TANK
          The leader of every ship is given the
          codes to Zion's mainframe computer.
          If an Agent had those codes and got
          inside Zion's mainframe, they could
          destroy us.

He looks up at Trinity who is pacing relentlessly.

                    TANK
          We can't let that happen, Trinity.
          Zion is more important than me. Or
          you or even Morpheus.

Trinity sees Cypher's dead body. Rage overtakes her and she
kicks him.

                    TRINITY
          Goddamnit! Goddamnit!

                    NEO
          There has to be something that we
          can do.

                    TANK
          There is. We have to pull the
          plug.

                    TRINITY
          You're going to kill him? Kill
          Morpheus?!

                    TANK
          Trinity, we don't have any other
          choice.

142   **INT. GOVERNMENT BUILDING**   142

Morpheus is fighting to hold his mind together. The Agents
stand over him.

                    AGENT SMITH
          Never send a human to do a
          machine's job.

> AGENT BROWN
> If, indeed, the insider has
> failed, they will sever the
> connection as soon as possible,
> unless--

> AGENT JONES
> They are dead. In either case--

> AGENT SMITH
> We have no choice but to continue
> as planned. Deploy the sentinels.
> Immediately.

143   **INT. MAIN DECK**   **143**

Tank kneels beside Morpheus's body.

Neo suddenly sees it perfectly clear, fate rushing at him
like an oncoming train.

> TANK
> Morpheus, you were more than our
> leader. You were... our father.
> We will miss you, always.

Trinity can't bear to watch. As she closes her eyes, her
tears slip free.

Tank closes his eyes and takes hold of the plug.

Neo is paralyzed, his whole life is suddenly suspended by the
finality of this moment hurling at him with the speed of a
bullet.

> NEO
> Stop!

They both look at him.

> NEO
> Goddamnit! I don't believe this is
> happening!

> TANK
> Neo, this has to be done!

> NEO
> Does it? I don't know. This can't
> be just coincidence. It can't be!
> Can it?

> TANK
> What are you talking about?

                    NEO
          The Oracle. She told me this would
          happen. She told me...

Neo stops, his stare fixed on Morpheus.

                    NEO
          That I would have to make a
          choice...

                    TRINITY
          What choice?

He makes his choice. Turning, he walks to his chair.

                    TRINITY
          What are you doing?

                    NEO
          I'm going in.

                    TRINITY
          You can't!

                    NEO
          I have to.

                    TRINITY
          Morpheus sacrificed himself so we
          could get you out! There's no way
          you're going back in!

                    NEO
          Morpheus did what he did because
          he believed that I'm something I'm
          not.

                    TRINITY
          What?

                    NEO
          I'm not the One, Trinity. The
          Oracle hit me with that too.

Trinity is stunned.

                    TRINITY
          No, you... have to be.

                    NEO
          I'm sorry, I'm not. I'm just
          another guy. Morpheus is the one
          that matters.

                    TRINITY
          No, Neo. That's not true. It can't
          be true.

                    NEO
          Why?

                    TRINITY
          Because...

Uncertainty swallows her words and she is unable to tell him
what she wants to.

                    TANK
          Neo, this is loco. They've got
          Morpheus in a military-controlled
          building. Even if you somehow got
          inside, those are Agents holding
          him. Three of them! I want
          Morpheus back, too, but what you
          are talking about is suicide.

                    NEO
          I know that's what it looks like,
          but it's not. I can't logically
          explain to you why it's not.
          Morpheus believed something and he
          was ready to give his life for
          what he believed. I understand
          that now. That's why I have to go.

                    TANK
          Why?

                    NEO
          Because I believe in something.

                    TRINITY
          What?

                    NEO
          I believe I can bring him back.

Trinity stares at him, hovering on the edge that he just
jumped off. Her jaw sets and she starts climbing into the
chair beside him.

                    NEO
          What are you doing?

                    TRINITY
          I'm coming with you.

                    NEO
          No, you're not.

                    TRINITY
          No? Let me tell you what I
          believe. I believe Morpheus means
          more to me than he does to you.
          I believe that if you are serious
          about saving him then you are going
          to need my help and since I am the
          ranking officer on this ship, if
          you don't like it then I believe
          that you can go to hell, because
          you aren't going anywhere else.

There is nothing more to say except--

                    TRINITY
          Tank, load us up.

144   **INT. EXECUTIVE OFFICE - DAY**   144

Agent Smith sits casually across from Morpheus who is hunched
over, his body leaking and twitching.

                    AGENT SMITH
          I'd like to share a revelation
          that I've had during my time here.
          It came to me when I tried to
          classify your species. I've
          realized that you are not actually
          mammals.

The life signs continue their chaotic patterns.

                    AGENT SMITH
          Every mammal on this planet
          instinctively develops a natural
          equilibrium with the surrounding
          environment. But you humans do
          not. You move to an area and you
          multiply and multiply until every
          natural resource is consumed and
          the only way you can survive is to
          spread to another area.

He leans forward.

                    AGENT SMITH
          There is another organism on this
          planet that follows the same
          pattern. Do you know what it is? A
          virus.

He smiles.

                    AGENT SMITH
              Human beings are a disease, a
              cancer of this planet. You are a
              plague. And we are... the cure.

A144   INT. CONSTRUCT   A144

     Neo and Trinity stand in the white space of the construct as
     he answers his ringing cell phone.

                    TANK (V.O.)
              Okay. What do you need? Besides a
              miracle...

                    NEO
              Guns. Lots of guns.

145   INT. MAIN DECK   145

     Neo and Trinity's bodies hang motionless in their drive
     chairs as Tank hits load.

146   INT. CONSTRUCT   146

     Racks of weapons appear and they begin to arm themselves.

                    TRINITY
              No one has ever done anything like
              this.

                    NEO
              Yeah?

     He snap cocks an Uzi.

                    NEO
              That's why it's going to work.

147   INT. EXECUTIVE OFFICE - DAY   147

     Agent Smith is again at the window.

                    AGENT SMITH
              Why isn't the serum working?

                    AGENT BROWN
              Perhaps we are asking the wrong
              questions.

     Agent Smith hides his knotting fist. He is becoming angry. It
     is something that isn't supposed to happen to Agents.

                    AGENT SMITH
              Leave me with him.

Agents Brown and Jones look at each other.

                    AGENT SMITH
          Now!

They leave and Agent Smith sits beside Morpheus.

                    AGENT SMITH
          Can you hear me, Morpheus? I'm
          going to be honest with you.

He removes his earphone, letting it dangle over his shoulder.

                    AGENT SMITH
          I hate this place. This zoo. This
          prison. This reality, whatever you
          want to call it, I can't stand it
          any longer.

                    AGENT SMITH
          It's the smell, if there is such a
          thing. I feel saturated by it. I
          can taste your stink and every
          time I do, I fear that I've
          somehow been infected by it.

He wipes sweat from Morpheus's forehead, coating the tips of
his fingers, holding them to Morpheus's nose.

                    AGENT SMITH
          Repulsive, isn't it?

He lifts Morpheus's head, holding it tightly with both hands.

                    AGENT SMITH
          I must get out of here, I must get
          free. In this mind is the key. My
          key.

Morpheus sneers through his pain.

                    AGENT SMITH
          Once Zion is destroyed, there is
          no need for me to be here. Do you
          understand? I need the codes. I
          have to get inside Zion. You have
          to tell me how.

He begins squeezing, his fingers gouging into his flesh.

                    AGENT SMITH
          You are going to tell me or you
          are going to die.

Tank sits down beside Morpheus whose face is ashen like someone near death. He takes hold of his hand.

> TANK
> Hold on, Morpheus. They're coming
> for you. They're coming.

A dark wind blows.

In long black coats, Trinity and Neo push through the revolving doors.

Neo is carrying a duffel bag. Trinity has a large metal suitcase. They cut across the lobby to the security station, drawing nervous glances.

Dark glasses, game faces.

Neo calmly passes through the metal detector which begins to wail immediately. A security guard moves over toward Neo, raising his metal detection wand.

> GUARD
> Would you please remove any
> metallic items you are carrying:
> keys, loose change--

Neo slowly sets down his duffel bag and throws open his coat, revealing an arsenal of guns, knives, and grenades slung from a climbing harness.

> GUARD
> Holy shit--

Neo is a blur of motion. In a split second, three guards are dead before they hit the ground.

A fourth guard dives for cover, clutching his radio.

> GUARD 4
> Backup! Send in the backup!

He looks up as Trinity sets off the metal detector. It is the last thing he sees.

The backup arrives. A wave of soldiers blocking the elevators. The concrete cavern of the lobby becomes a white noise roar of gunfire.

Slate walls and pillars pock, crack, and crater under a hail swarm of explosive tipped bullets.

They are met by the quivering spit of a subhandmachine gun and the razored whistle of throwing knives. Weapons like extensions of their bodies are used with the same deadly precision as their feet and their fists.

Bodies slump down to the marbled floor while Neo and Trinity hardly even break their stride.

151   INT. EXECUTIVE OFFICE   151

Agents Jones and Brown burst into the room. Agent Smith releases Morpheus.

                    AGENT BROWN
               What were you doing?

Agent Smith recovers, replacing his ear-piece.

                    AGENT JONES
               You don't know.

                    AGENT SMITH
               Know what?

Agent Smith listens to his earphone, not believing what he is hearing.

152   INT. ELEVATORS - DAY   152

They get in. Trinity immediately drops and opens the suitcase, wiring a plastique and napalm bomb.

Neo hits the emergency stop. He pulls down part of the false ceiling and finds the elevator shaft access panel.

153   INT. EXECUTIVE OFFICE - DAY   153

Agent Jones looks at Morpheus.

                    AGENT JONES
               I think they're trying to save
               him.

154   INT. ELEVATOR SHAFT - DAY   154

Neo ratchets down a clamp onto the elevator cable. Both of them lock on. He looks up the long, dark throat of the building and takes a deep breath.

                    NEO
               There is no spoon.

Neo whips out his gun and presses it to the cable, lower than they attached themselves.

BOOM! The cable snaps.

The counter-weights plummet, yanking Trinity and Neo up through the shaft as the elevator falls away beneath them, distending space, filling it with the sound of whistling metal as they soar to the top.

155   INT. LOBBY - DAY   155

The elevator hits the bottom.

BA-BOOM!

The massive explosion blows open the doors, fire clouds engulfing the elevator section of the lobby.

156   INT. EXECUTIVE OFFICE - DAY   156

The Agents hear the blast of fire alarms.

                    AGENT JONES
              Lower level--

                    AGENT BROWN
              They are actually attacking.

Another enormous explosion thunders above them, shaking the building. The alarm sounds, emergency sprinklers begin showering the room.

Agent Smith smashes a table.

                    AGENT SMITH
              Find them and destroy them!

Agent Jones nods and touches his ear-piece.

157   EXT. ROOF - DAY   157

The roof-access tower is now engulfed in flames as Neo and Trinity stand amongst a pile of their fallen enemies.

Across the roof, the pilot inside the army helicopter watches the last of their ferocious onslaught.

                    PILOT
              I repeat, we are under attack!

Suddenly his face, his whole body dissolves, consumed by spreading locust-like swarm of static as Agent Jones emerges.

100

Just as she drops the final Marine, Trinity sees what's coming. Neo sees her, the fear in her face, and he knows what is behind him.

Screaming, he whirls, guns filling his hands with thought-speed.

Fingers pumping, shells ejecting, dancing up and away, we look through the sights and gunsmoke at the Agent blurred with motion--

Until the hammers click against the empty metal.

                    NEO
          Trinity!

Agent Jones charges.

                    NEO
          ...help.

His gun booms as we enter the liquid space of--

Bullet-time.

The air sizzles with wads of lead like angry flies as Neo twists, bends, ducks just between them.

Agent Jones still running, narrows the gap, the bullets coming faster until Neo bent impossibly back, one hand on the ground as a spiraling gray ball shears open his shoulder.

He starts to scream as another digs a red groove across his thigh. He has only time to look up, to see Agent Jones standing over him, raising his gun a final time.

                    AGENT JONES
          Only human...

Suddenly Agent Jones stops. He hears a sharp metal click.

Immediately, he whirls around and turns straight into the muzzle of Trinity's .45--

Jammed tight to his head.

                    TRINITY
          Dodge this!

BOOM! BOOM! BOOM! The body flies back with a flash of mercurial light and when it hits the ground, it is the pilot.

Trinity helps Neo up.

                    TRINITY
          Neo, how did you do that?

101

                    NEO
          Do what?

                    TRINITY
          You moved like they moved. I've
          never seen anyone move that fast.
                    NEO
          It wasn't fast enough.

He checks his shoulder wound.

                    TRINITY
          Are you all right?

                    NEO
          I'm fine. Come on, we have to keep
          moving.

Neo sees the helicopter.

                    NEO
          Can you fly that thing?

                    TRINITY
          Not yet.

She pulls out the cellular phone.

158   INT. HOVERCRAFT   158

Tank is back at the controls.

                    TANK
          Operator.

                    TRINITY (V.O.)
          Tank, I need a pilot program for a
          military B-212 helicopter.

Tank is immediately searching the disk drawers.

                    TRINITY (V.O.)
          Hurry!

His fingers flash over the gleaming laser disks finding one
that he feeds into Trinity's Supplement Drive punching the
"load" commands on her keyboard.

159   EXT. ROOF - DAY   159

Trinity's eyes flutter as information surges into her brain,
all the essentials of flying a helicopter absorbed at light-
speed.

                            TRINITY
                      Let's go.

160   SCENE OMITTED   160

161   INT. EXECUTIVE OFFICE - DAY   161

         Agent Jones throws open the door and enters, walking through
         the puddles pooling in the carpet. Over the rushing water and
         the alarms, Agent Smith hears a sound and understands the
         seriousness of the attack.

         He turns to the wall of windows as the helicopter drops into
         view--

         Neo is in the back bay, aiming the mounted .50 machine gun.

                            AGENT SMITH
                      No.

         The gun jumps and bullets explode through the window in a
         cacophony of crashing glass as the Agents go for their
         weapons.

         But Neo is too close, the .50 caliber too fast and bullets
         are everywhere, perforating the room.

         Agent Jones is hit first, his body jack-knifing back, blood
         arcing out with a sudden flash of light--

         Then Agent Brown, his gun still firing as his body falls. And
         finally Agent Smith.

         Neo stares at Morpheus, trying to will him into action.

                            NEO
                      Get up, Morpheus! Get up!

         Neo grabs the climbing rope and attaches one end to his
         harness.

162   INT. HALL - DAY   162

         Just outside the executive office, three Marines blister with
         snow-static.

163   INT. EXECUTIVE OFFICE - DAY   163

         Slowly, Morpheus lifts his face into the room's rain. When he
         finally opens his eyes, they are again dark and flashing with
         fire.

         He rises from the chair, snapping his handcuffs just as the
         Agents enter the adjoining room. Agent Smith stops and sees
         Morpheus run past the open door.

                                                          103

                    AGENT SMITH
              Nooo!

He fires sweeping across the sheetrocked wall in a perfect
line.

For an instant, we see the bullets shred, puncturing the
wall, searing through the wet air with jet trails of chalk.

And as Morpheus starts his dive for the window, a bullet
buries itself in his leg, knocking him off balance.

                    NEO
              He won't make it.

Morpheus lunges, out of control--

As Neo spins, every move a whip crack, snapping the other
rope-end on to a bolted bar as--

Morpheus begins to fall, when Neo hurls himself into the wide
blue empty space, flying for a moment.

The rope snaking out behind him; an umbilical cord attached
to a machine.

As their two bodies, set in motion, rushing at each other on
a seemingly magnetic course until they collide.

Almost bouncing free of each other, arms, legs scrambling,
hands searching in furious desperation, finding hold and
clinging.

Until the line ends, snapping taut, cracking their fragile
embrace. Morpheus tumbles, legs flipping over, falling down--

The ground deliriously distant as Neo snatches hold of his
mentor's still handcuffed wrist.

                    NEO
              Gotcha!

164   **EXT. GOVERNMENT BUILDING - DAY**   164

Trinity pulls the copter up and away as Agent Smith stands in
the shattered window, aiming his gun out through the curtain
of rain.

Ponk. Ponk. Ponk. The rear hull is punched full of holes and
smoke and oil pour out like black blood.

                    TRINITY
              Shit-shit-no!

Neo hears the helicopter begin to die.

                    NEO
              Uh oh--

Trinity throws the helicopter towards the roof of the nearest
building.

Morpheus and Neo cling to one another as they and the machine
above them begin to fall.

The engine grinds, the chopping blades start to slow while--

Trinity guides the parabolic fall over the nearest roof where--

Neo and Morpheus drop safely, rolling free as the rope goes
slack. Neo gets to his feet, trying to detach himself but--

The helicopter is falling too fast, arcing over the roof like
a setting sun--

The coils of slack snap taut, yanking Neo off his feet,
dragging him with ferocious speed towards the edge even as--

Trinity lunges for the back door, her gun in one hand,
grabbing for the rope with the other--

Neo flies like a skipping stone, hurtling at the parapet,
when his feet hit the rain gutter and he levers up just as--

Trinity fires, severing the cord from the helicopter, falling
free of it as it smashes, blades first into a glass
skyscraper.

Holding onto the rope as she swings, connected to Neo, who
stands on the building's edge watching her arc beneath him as
the helicopter explodes--

She bounces against a shatterproof window that spider-cracks
out while flames erupt behind her.

165   **INT. MAIN DECK**   165

Tank stares at the screen, his mouth agape.

                    TANK
              I knew it! He's the One.

166   **SCENE OMITTED**   166

167   **EXT. ROOFTOP - DAY**   167

Neo pulls Trinity up into his arms. Both shaking, they hold
each other again.

                    MORPHEUS
          Do you believe it now, Trinity?

Trinity looks at Neo.

                    NEO
          Morpheus, the Oracle... she told
          me--

                    MORPHEUS
          She told you exactly what you
          needed to hear. That's all. Sooner
          or later, Neo, you're going to
          realize just like I did the
          difference between knowing a path
          and walking a path.

168   **INT. MAIN DECK**   168

     The phone rings.

                    MORPHEUS (V.O.)
          Tank.

                    TANK
          Goddamn! It's good to hear your
          voice, sir!

                    MORPHEUS (V.O.)
          We need an exit.

                    TANK
          Got one ready, sir. Subway. State
          and Balbo.

                    MORPHEUS (V.O.)
          We're on our way--

169   **EXT. ROOFTOP - DAY**   169

     We rush at the roof access door as it suddenly slams open and
     the three Agents charge out. But Neo, Trinity, and Morpheus
     are already gone.

                    AGENT SMITH
          Damnit!

                    AGENT BROWN
          The trace was completed.

                    AGENT JONES
          We have their position.

AGENT BROWN
Sentinels are standing by.

AGENT JONES
Order the strike.

Agent Smith can't stand listening to them. He moves to the
edge of the building, looking out at the surrounding city.

AGENT SMITH
They're not out yet.

170   INT. SUBWAY STATION - DAY   170

An old man sits hunched in the far corner of the station,
shadows gathered around him like blankets. Mumbling, he
nurses from a bottle of Thunderbird when--

A phone begins to ring.

Neo leads Trinity and Morpheus bounding over a set of
turnstiles towards the ringing phone inside a graffiti-
covered booth.

NEO
Let's go! You first, Morpheus.

Morpheus gets in and answers the phone.

Lost in the shadow, the Old Man watches as Morpheus
disappears, the phone dropping, dangling by its cord. His
eyes grow wide, glowing white in the dark.

171   EXT. ROOFTOP - DAY   171

Agent Smith stares, his face twisted with hate. He will never
be free of the Matrix.

He starts to turn from the edge of the building when he
suddenly hears it, his head whipping back around, staring--

172   INT. SUBWAY - DAY   172

Through the Old Man's eyes as the world begins to rumble.

Trinity hangs up the phone, then turns to Neo.

The rumble grows, the ground beginning to shake.

TRINITY
Neo, I want to tell you
something... but I'm afraid of
what it could mean if I do.

Behind her, the phone begins to ring.

                    TRINITY
        Everything the Oracle told me, has
        come true, everything but this...

                    NEO
        But what?

The rumble rises, drowning her voice. Neo is drawn towards
her, their lips close enough to kiss when a train blasts into
the station.

For a moment, they are frozen by the strobing lights of the
train until Trinity turns, unable to say what she wants to
say.

The phone rings once more before she lifts the receiver when,
in the darkness of the far corner, Neo sees the old man in
the flashing train-light as he becomes--

Agent Smith, raising a fistful of black gun-metal.

                    NEO
            No!

The gun fires, the bullet flying at her, bursting through the
plastic window just as Trinity disappears.

The handset hanging in the air as the bullet hits, shattering
the ear-piece.

173   INT. HOVERCRAFT   **173**

Trinity blinks, shivering as her conscious exits the
Construct.

                    TRINITY
            Neo!

                    TANK
        What the hell just happened?

                    TRINITY
        An Agent! You have to send me
        back!

                    TANK
            I can't!

174   INT. SUBWAY STATION - DAY   **174**

The destroyed phone dangles in the empty booth. Neo turns to
Agent Smith whose gun stares at him like a third eye.

                          AGENT SMITH
                       Mr. Anderson.

175   INT. MAIN DECK   175

Morpheus and Trinity stand behind Tank riveted to the
scrolling code.

                          TRINITY
                       Run, Neo. Run.

176   INT. SUBWAY STATION - DAY   176

Neo looks at the dead escalator that rises up behind him.
Slowly he turns back and in his eyes we see something
different, something fixed and hard like a gunfighter's
resolve.

There is no past or future in these eyes. There is only what
is.

177   INT. MAIN DECK   177

Trinity is unable to understand.

                          TRINITY
                       What is he doing?

                          MORPHEUS
                    He's beginning to believe.

178   INT. SUBWAY STATION - DAY   178

Neo whip-draws his gun flashpoint speed of lightning as--

Smith opens fire.

Gun report thunders through the underground, both men
blasting, moving at impossible speed.

For a blinking moment we enter Bullet-time.

Gun flash tongues curl from Neo's gun, bullets float forward
like a plane moving across the sky, cartridges cartwheel into
space.

An instant later they are nearly on top of each other,
rolling up out of a move that is almost a mirrored reflection
of the other--

Each jamming their gun tight to the other's head.

They freeze in a kind of embrace; Neo sweating, panting,
Agent Smith machine-calm. Agent Smith smiles.

                         AGENT SMITH
                    You're empty.

Neo pulls the trigger. Click.

                            NEO
                    So are you.

The smile falls. Agent Smith yanks his trigger.

CLICK.

Agent Smith's face warps with rage and he attacks, fists
flying at furious speed, blows and counters, Neo retreating
as--

A knife-hand opens his forearm, and a kick sends him slamming
back against a steel column. Stunned, he ducks just under a
punch that crunches into the beam, steel chunks exploding
like shrapnel.

Behind him, Neo leaps into the air, delivering a neck-
snapping reverse round-house. Agent Smith's glasses fly off
and he glares at Neo; his eyes ice blue.

                         AGENT SMITH
                    I'm going to enjoy watching you
                    die, Mr. Anderson.

Agent Smith attacks with unrelenting fury, fists pounding Neo
like jackhammers.

179   INT. HOVERCRAFT   179

        Trinity watches Neo as his body jerks, mouth coughing blood,
        his life signs going wild.

                            TRINITY
                    Jesus, he's killing him!

180   INT. SUBWAY STATION - DAY   180

        Agent Smith grabs hold of him, lifting him into the air,
        hurling him against the curved wall of the train tunnel,
        where he falls inches from the electrified third-rail.

        The Agent is about to jump down and press his attack when he
        hears something. From deep in the tunnel, like an animal cry,
        a burst of high-speed metal grinding against metal.

        The sound of an oncoming train.

110

Neo tries to get up. Agent Smith jumps down onto the tracks and drop-kicks him in the face. The world again begins to shake, rumbling as the train nears.

> AGENT SMITH
> Do you hear that, Mr. Anderson?

Agent Smith grabs Neo in a choke-hold forcing him to look down the tracks, the train's headlight burning a hole in the darkness.

> AGENT SMITH
> That is the sound of
> inevitability.

Neo sees it coming and he starts to fight.

> AGENT SMITH
> It is the sound of your death.

There is another metal screech, much louder, closer, as Agent Smith tightens his hold. Neo is unable to breathe.

> AGENT SMITH
> Good-bye, Mr. Anderson.

The train roars at them, swallowing Agent Smith's words. The veins bulge in Neo's head, as he grits through the pain.

He is not ready to die.

> NEO
> My name is Neo.

Impossibly, he hurls himself straight up, smashing Smith against the concrete ceiling of the tunnel.

They fall as the sound and fury of the train explodes into the station. Neo backflips up off the tracks just as--

The train barrels over Agent Smith.

Neo stands, knees shaking, when the train slams on its emergency brake. With an ear-splitting shriek of tortured rails, the train slows, part of it still in the station.

Neo turns, limping, starting to run, racing for the escalator--

As the train comes to a stop and the doors of the last car open; Agent Smith bursts out in furious pursuit, his glasses again intact.

Tank searches the Matrix.

> TRINITY
> What just happened?

> TANK
> I don't know. I lost him.

> MORPHEUS
> He's on the run--

Suddenly, a siren sounds.

> TANK
> Oh shit!

Morpheus bolts to the ladder.

Morpheus climbs into the cockpit. On the hologram radar, he sees the Sentinels.

> TRINITY
> Oh no.

Trinity is behind him.

> TRINITY
> How long?

> MORPHEUS
> Five minutes. Maybe six.

Morpheus lifts the headset.

> MORPHEUS
> Tank, charge the E.M.P.

> TANK (V.O.)
> Yes, sir.

> TRINITY
> You can't use that until Neo is
> out!

> MORPHEUS
> I know, Trinity. Don't worry. He's
> going to make it.

EXT. CITY STREET - DAY   183

A BUSINESSMAN walks along the sidewalk, wheeling and dealing
into his cell phone when it disappears, snatched by Neo as he
flashes by.

> MAN
> What the shit-- My phone!

The man turns to call for help and when he turns back, it is
Agent Smith.

Neo is in a full-out sprint, spinning and weaving away from
every pedestrian, every potential Agent. He flips open the
cell phone and dials long distance.

184   **INT. HOVERCRAFT**   184

Tank answers.

> TANK
> Operator.

> NEO (V.O.)
> Mr. Wizard, get me the hell out of
> here!

185   **EXT. CITY STREET - DAY**   185

Neo dives down an alley, Agent Smith starting to gain.

> NEO
> Hurry, Tank! I got some serious
> pursuit!

186   **INT. HOVERCRAFT**   186

The keyboard clicking, Tank searches for an exit. Trinity
screams into the headset.

> TRINITY
> Neo, you better get your ass back
> here!

187   **EXT. ALLEY**   187

Agent Smith stops and takes aim.

> NEO
> I'm trying, Trinity. I'm trying.

A bullet shatters the image of Neo in a truck's rearview
mirror.

188   INT. MAIN DECK   188

        Tank speed-reads the reams of Matrix code.

                        TANK
                I got a patch on an old exit.
                Wabash and Lake. A hotel. Room
                303.

189   SCENE OMITTED   189

190   EXT. OPEN MARKET   190

        Neo spins away, turning and finds himself in an open market
        that teems with people.

        He kamikazes his way down the little avenues lined with
        vendors and shops, careening through the labyrinth, out of
        control. And at every turn there is an Agent, appearing from
        crowds, behind fish counters, tent flaps, and crates.

191   SCENE OMITTED   191

192   EXT. ALLEY   192

        He dives from the maze down a service alley but it is a dead
        end.

        Neo turns back as the Agents emerge from the market.

                        NEO
                Uh, help! Need a little help!

193   INT. MAIN DECK   193

        Tank frantically scans the monitor like a road map.

                        TANK
                The door.

194   EXT. ALLEY   194

        Neo dives for it but--

                        NEO
                It's locked.

                        TANK (V.O.)
                Kick it in!

        Peeling back, Neo almost kicks the door from its hinges,
        lunging from the Agents' bullets.

195   INT. APARTMENT BUILDING - STAIRCASE   195

        Neo springs up the old crooked apartment building stairs.

INT. APARTMENT BUILDING - HALL

He is halfway down the hall, running in sharp long strides when a door explodes open at the end.

> TANK (V.O.)
> Shit! The door on your left.

Neo lurches, kicking in an apartment door.

> TANK (V.O.)
> No! Other left!

He whirls back to his other left, battering through the door which splinters, perforated by bullets.

An old woman watches TV as Neo blurs past her and into her kitchen, where another woman is chopping vegetables.

> TANK (V.O.)
> That window!

Neo throws it open, leaping for the fire escape just as a knife buries itself in the window casing.

> TANK (V.O.)
> Down! Down!

B195   **EXT. APARTMENT BUILDING - FIRE ESCAPE**   **B195**

Tumbling down the rattling fire escape, Neo leaps the last ten feet into the alley below with Agent Brown right behind him.

Neo scrapes himself to his feet, broken and bleeding, charging for the end of the alley.

196   **INT. MAIN DECK**   **196**

Finger on the monitor, Tank traces Neo's path.

> TANK
> That's it! You're almost there!
> That fire escape at the end of the
> alley!

197   **EXT. HEART O' THE CITY HOTEL - DAY**   **197**

Agent Smith suddenly pauses as if recognizing something; the faded neon buzzes: Heart O' The City Hotel.

198   **INT. HOVERCRAFT**   **198**

Tank loads the exit.

                              TANK
                    I'm going to make the call.

                             MORPHEUS
                    Do it!

Suddenly, the lights go red.

                             TRINITY
                         No.

Morpheus looks up.

                             MORPHEUS
                    Here they come.

199   EXT. SEWER MAIN   **199**

The Sentinels open and shift like killer kaleidoscopes as
they attack, slamming down onto the Nebuchadnezzar.

200   INT. HOVERCRAFT   **200**

The hovercraft booms down as they hit. Morpheus opens the
lock on the E.M.P. detonator.

Trinity watches him.

                             MORPHEUS
                    He's going to make it.

201   EXT. ALLEY - DAY   **201**

Neo scrambles up the fire escape, bullets sparking and
ricocheting around him as Agents Brown and Jones close the
gap.

A201   INT. HALL - DAY   **A201**

On the third floor, he kicks in the window, jumping into the
hall. The doors count backwards: 310... 309...

202   INT. MAIN DECK   **202**

Another systems alarm sounds.

                              TANK
                    They've burned through the outer
                    hull.

                             TRINITY
                    Hurry, Neo.

116

203   INT. HALL - DAY   203

       Neo can hear the phone ringing. 305... 304...

       Agent Brown reaches the broken window behind him just as Neo
       grabs the handle of 303, throwing open the door to find--

       Agent Smith, waiting, .45 cocked.

       Neo can't move-- can't think--

       BOOM.

204   INT. MAIN DECK   204

       Neo's body jerks, and everyone hears it as the life monitors
       snap flatline.

       Trinity screams. Morpheus stumbles back in disbelief.

                         MORPHEUS
                 No, it can't be. It can't be.

       Lasers suddenly sear through the main deck as the Sentinels
       slice open the hull.

205   INT. HALL - DAY   205

       Three holes in his chest, Neo falls to the blue shag
       carpeting, blood smearing down the wallpaper. Agent Smith
       stands over him, still aiming, taking no chances.

                         AGENT SMITH
                 Check him.

206   INT. MAIN DECK   206

       Amid the destruction raining around her, Trinity takes hold
       of Neo's body.

                         TRINITY
                 Neo...

207   INT. HALL - DAY   207

       Kneeling beside him, Agent Brown checks his vital signs.

                         AGENT BROWN
                 He's gone.

       Agent Smith smiles, standing over him.

                         AGENT SMITH
                 Good-bye, Mr. Anderson.

In tears, Morpheus takes hold of the E.M.P. switch.

Trinity whispers in Neo's ear.

> TRINITY
> Neo, please, listen to me. I
> promised to tell you the rest. The
> Oracle, she told me that I'd fall
> in love and that man, the man I
> loved would be the One. You see?
> You can't be dead, Neo, you can't
> be because I love you. You hear
> me? I love you!

Her eyes close and she kisses him, believing in all her heart
that he will feel her lips and know that they speak the
truth.

209   INT. HOTEL HALL - DAY   209

He does. And they do.

His eyes snap open.

210   INT. MAIN DECK   210

Trinity screams as the monitors jump back to life. Tank and
Morpheus look at each other.

It is a miracle.

> TRINITY
> Now get up!

211   INT. HALL - DAY   211

Holding his chest, Neo struggles to get up. At the end of the
hall, the Agents wait for the elevator when Agent Smith
glances back. He rips off his sunglasses looking at Neo as if
he were looking at a ghost.

Neo gets to his feet all three Agents grabbing for their
guns. As one, they fire.

> NEO
> No!

Neo raises his hands and the bullets, like a cloud of
obedient bees, slow and come to a stop. They hang frozen in
space, fixed like stainless steel stars.

The Agents are unable to absorb what they are seeing.

Neo plucks one of the bullets from the air. We see him and the hall reflected in the bright casing. We move closer until the bullet fills our vision and the distorted reflection morphs, becoming the 'real' image.

He drops the bullet and the others fall to the floor.

Neo looks out, now able to see through the curtain of the Matrix. For a moment, the walls, the floor, even the Agents become a rushing stream of code.

212   **INT. MAIN DECK**   212

All three stare transfixed with awe as the scrolling code accelerates, faster and faster, as if the machine language was unable to keep up or perhaps describe what is happening.

They begin to blur into streaks, shimmering ribbons of light that open like windows, as--

Each screen fills with brilliant saturated color images of Neo standing in the hall.

                    TANK
               How...?!

                    MORPHEUS
               He is the One. He is the One!

An explosion shakes the entire ship.

213   **INT. HALL**   213

Agent Smith screams, his calm machine-like expression shredding with pure rage.

He rushes Neo. His attack is ferocious but Neo blocks each blow easily. Then with one quick strike to the chest he sends Agent Smith flying backwards.

For the first time since their inception, the Agents know fear.

Agent Smith gets up, bracing himself as Neo charges him and springs into a dive. But the impact doesn't come. Neo sinks into Agent Smith, disappearing, his tie and coat rippling as if he were a deep pool of water.

Spinning around he looks to the others and feels something, like a tremor before a quake, something deep, something that is going to change everything.

Suddenly a searing sound stabs through his ear-piece as his chest begins to swell, then balloon as--

Neo bursts up out of him. And with a final death scream, Agent Smith explodes like an empty husk in a brilliant cacophony of light, his shards spinning away, absorbed by the Matrix until--

Only Neo is left.

Neo faces the remaining Agents. They look at each other, the same idea striking simultaneously--

They run.

214   **INT. MAIN DECK**   214

Sentinels are everywhere destroying the ship.

                         TRINITY
                Neo!

215   **INT. HALL**   215

Again he hears her. He reacts to the ringing phone, rushing towards it even as--

216   **INT. MAIN DECK**   216

A Sentinel descends towards Morpheus. On the screen we see Neo dive for the phone.

                         TRINITY
                Now!

Morpheus turns the key.

217   **INT. OVERFLOW PIT**   217

A blinding shock of white light floods the chamber; Sentinels blink and fall instantly dead, filling the pit with their cold metal carcasses.

218   **INT. HOVERCRAFT**   218

In the still darkness, only the humans are alive.

                         TRINITY
                Neo?

His eyes open. Tears pour from her smiling eyes as he reaches up to touch her.

And she kisses him; it seems like it might last forever.

                                        FADE TO BLACK.

Close on a computer screen as in the opening. The cursor
beating steadily, waiting. A phone begins to ring.

It is answered and the screen fills instantly with the trace
program. After a long beat, we recognize Neo's voice.

              NEO (V.O.)
        Hi. It's me. I know you're out
        there. I can feel you now.

We close in on the racing columns of numbers shimmering
across the screen.

              NEO (V.O.)
        I imagine you can also feel me.

The numbers begin to lock into place.

              NEO (V.O.)
        You won't have to search for me
        anymore. I'm done running. Done
        hiding. Whether I'm done fighting,
        I suppose, is up to you.

We glide in towards the screen.

              NEO (V.O.)
        I believe deep down, we both want
        this world to change. I believe
        that the Matrix can remain our
        cage or it can become our
        chrysalis, that's what you helped
        me to understand. That to be free,
        truly free, you cannot change your
        cage. You have to change yourself.

We dive through the numbers, surging up through the darkness,
sucked towards a tight constellation of stars.

              NEO (V.O.)
        When I used to look out at this
        world, all I could see was its
        edges, its boundaries, its rules
        and controls, its leaders and
        laws. But now, I see another
        world. A different world where all
        things are possible. A world of
        hope. Of peace.

We realize that the constellation is actually the holes in
the mouthpiece of a phone. Seen from inside.

                              NEO (V.O.)
                    I can't tell you how to get there,
                    but I know if you can free your
                    mind, you'll find the way.

220   EXT. PHONE BOOTH/STREET   220

         We shoot through the holes as Neo hangs up the phone. He
         steps out of the phone and slides on a pair of sunglasses. He
         looks up and we rise.

         Higher and higher, until the city is miles below.

         After a moment, Neo blasts by us, his long black coat
         billowing like a black leather cape as he flies faster than a
         speeding bullet.

                                                  FADE OUT.

SCENE NOTES

This is the part of the book usually written by the directors. They give their comments on how they shot certain scenes, what scenes broke their hearts when they had to be cut, and why they wrote the script in the first place. On top of that, they might give funny anecdotes about what happened to them while they were making the film: heartwarming stories like how they got through the trying times when they thought it was never going to happen and the pure elation they felt when the film was finally released to widespread critical acclaim and box office success. After reading a section like this, you feel somehow closer to the directors, like you've taken the journey with them.

That's how it usually works.

Larry and Andy, however, were too busy so they asked me to do it. I was their assistant on *The Matrix* so, basically, I spent every moment with them while they were making the film. I saw the whole process, from the first draft of the script, to the completion of the storyboards (which eventually convinced Warner Bros. to make the film), to the casting process, then preproduction, principal photography, editing, all the way through the final sound mix. When you consider that, it is almost like they wrote this section . . . or maybe not. Anyway, I gave it my best shot. I hope you enjoy it.

—Phil Oosterhouse, 2000

PHIL OOSTERHOUSE was born in Grand Rapids, Michigan. After studying philosophy, English, and photography at Calvin College, he moved to Los Angeles. In LA, he spent some time writing and working until he took a job as Larry and Andy Wachowski's assistant on *Bound*. This job continued through production of *The Matrix*. For the sequels, he will be the Associate Producer.

Scene 2: TRINITY CHASE. Look for the map of Australia torn into the wallpaper.

Scene 4: TRINITY CHASE. This scene was the first of Carrie-Anne's wall running scenes. One of the most impressive things about the film was the actors' insane dedication to the kung fu training. Keanu, Laurence, Carrie-Anne, and Hugo all could have done two or three films in the time it took to train for and shoot *The Matrix*. Doing in six months what normally takes years, Yuen Wo Ping transformed four Hollywood actors into kung fu masters. This was the first scene with kung fu wire work that was shot. Carrie-Anne nailed it, putting the pressure on the other actors to do the same.

Scene 14: NEO'S APARTMENT. A lot of people have asked about the significance of the numbers that show up in the film. In this scene, the clock reads 9:18 because this is the birthday of Andy's wife.

Scene 15: CORTECHS CAPTURE. The addition of Meta to CorTechs saved us billions in lawsuits, or so we were told by the lawyers.

Scene 16: CORTECHS CAPTURE. For safety reasons, the window cleaners in this scene ended up being played by our stunt coordinator, Glenn Boswell, and stuntman, Lou Horvath. Be sure to notice their expert window cleaning technique.

Scene 17: CORTECHS CAPTURE. Day one of shooting. Everyone was nervous, all the Warner Bros. guys were out, making sure Larry and Andy knew what they were doing. No one really knew how it was going to go. As it turned out, the day was flawless. The actors were fantastic, Larry and Andy got every setup they wanted and we finished on time.

Scene 18: CORTECHS CAPTURE. Complete contrast to Scene 17. The shot of the phone dropping took nearly half a day and wasn't used. It was reshot on a bluescreen stage. We ran out of sun at the end of the day and had to rebuild the office onstage to get the remaining interior setups. More kudos for Keanu's dedication, however: he was actually out on the ledge, thirty-four stories up because he wanted to be.

Scene 20: INTERROGATION ROOM. The bug went through many conceptions before the finished product. Like many of the CG creatures in this film, it took a long time to create a creature that looked like it belonged in the scene. There were countless conversations about details like tentacle motion (flailing or not) and the texture and opacity of the sac. In the film, you also might notice a difference in the prosthetic Neo stomach that the bug burrows into, and Keanu's stomach when the Agents rip open his shirt. The stomach model was made before Keanu was deep into training. Keanu warned us that his stomach would look nothing like that when we got to shooting, and he was right.

Scene 30: POWER PLANT. A great scene and another in which Keanu should be commended for his dedication. It was the last scene on the schedule because Keanu had to be shaved completely bald, including his eyebrows. He also lost considerable weight for this scene so that he looked like he'd been lying inactive in gel for years. If that wasn't enough, he had to spend four hours at the beginning of each day in prosthetic makeup as the jacks were put on his body. There were Internet rumors circulating throughout production that we had built a fully animatronic Keanu for this scene and the tougher action. That was untrue but there was a prosthetic Keanu head made for the close up of the Docbot removing the plug from his neck.

Scene 31: POWER PLANT. Three underwater camera housings were broken shooting this scene. There was one point in the waterslide in which the stuntman and cameraman built up so much speed that they slammed into the top of the tube, shattering the camera housing.

Scene 35: NEO WAKES UP. Eight hours of prosthetic makeup for this scene. Those are real acupuncture needles in Keanu's face and forehead. The needles were provided and placed by Longie, the cast masseur whose official title is Master of Pressure Points. Throughout the shoot, the cast would get worn down and Longie would be called in to heal their wounds. He was so effective that by the end of the shoot, they all would have joined a cult if Longie had told them to.

Scene 39: HISTORY PROGRAM. This scene was shot in a stage that was completely painted white. The cameramen wore white suits to cut down on reflection in Morpheus's glasses. The sunglasses presented constant reflection problems for Bill Pope, the director of photography. As a result, nearly every scene was a challenge and Bill conquered all of them. We'll see how he does on the sequels when everybody has a fully reflective chrome head.

Scene A40: HISTORY PROGRAM. A lot of people questioned how we got a baby to be so well behaved while shooting this scene, especially with a jack in the back of its neck. Fortunately, it isn't a real baby, just a very convincing prosthetic constructed by MEG in Australia.

Scene 48: CONSTRUCT KUNG FU. Again, the actors deserve credit for their preparation. This scene took a whole week to shoot. Laurence and Keanu had to do these moves take after take and they kicked ass despite the intense heat. Because Larry and Andy were shooting at speeds as high as 300fps, Bill Pope needed to use huge lights to get enough illumination. The lights gave off enormous amounts of heat and once even began to singe the rice paper on the dojo walls. Wo Ping did a great job choreographing this scene and his wire team did some amazing work as well. The most difficult wire work appears in this scene.

Scene 57: CONSTRUCT ROOFTOP. Larry and Andy couldn't find a section of Sydney big enough to create the effect of the city rushing up at their feet. Sydney just doesn't have the urban sprawl we have become accustomed to in America. In the early visual effects meetings when discussing how the shot should look, they described the city looking like a circuit board as it rushes up at Neo and Morpheus. So, John Gaeta took the existing helicopter shot of Sydney and merged it with a photo of an actual circuit board to fill in the gaps. If you step frame by frame through the final shot, you can actually see the circuit board mixed in with the city.

Scene 63: TRAINING PROGRAM. For the extras, Larry and Andy requested twins. We had multiple sets of real twins and triplets. To fill in the gaps, Manex created more to give the impression that Mouse got lazy and duplicated people instead of creating unique ones.

There was a funny moment involving the woman in the red dress, Fiona Johnson. She came by for a costume fitting and was waiting just outside the set for Larry and Andy to finish. Across the street, some guy pulling out of his garage was so distracted by her beauty that he actually drove his car through the garage door. The bottom of the door scraped over the entire length of his car, ruining his new paint job. The guy drove away humiliated, his windshield wipers twisted lamely out of position.

Scene 71: NEO TAKES A DRINK. The section where Cypher tells Neo there were five potential Ones before him was shot and then cut in postproduction for reasons only Larry and Andy know.

Scene A71: STEAK. This scene alternated between being cut, indispensable, moved around and then, finally, put back in its original position. It's a good scene, giving you more insight into why Cypher would sell everyone out. Plus, every time we did a take, they had to replace Cypher's steak and we got to eat the other ones. The steaks were provided by a restaurant called Level 41 and were probably the best in Sydney.

Scene 79: SPOON BOY. Rowan Witt, who played Spoon Boy, appears in *Dark City* with a shaved head as well. By the time we got around to casting *The Matrix*, his hair had grown back and he had long curly locks that his mother loved. He was cast as Spoon Boy and as it got closer and closer to shooting, his mother kept trying to convince Larry and Andy that maybe Spoon Boy didn't need to be bald. Eventually, she was convinced and on the day his head was shaved, his mother saved his hair in a plastic bag which Rowan carried around the set. In the end, he looked great and did a great job. Finally, in a testament to how long it took to complete this film, we saw the Witts again during postproduction while Rowan was shooting a commercial. His long curly locks had returned.

Bending spoons came courtesy of Dfilm.

Scene 87: DEJA VU. Great cat acting here. How did they get it to do exactly the same thing twice, complete with identical meows? Wow, that cat was good.

A lot of people have asked if the animals in the Matrix are also hooked up in pods. Unfortunately, they are not, they're all computer generated images.

Scenes 134/135: TV REPAIR SHOP. A great acting scene. I've been surprised by how many people identify with Cypher in this film, people who would rather live on in ignorant bliss if the Matrix was a reality. As for me, I imagine I couldn't get enough cold goop. The building this was shot in was allegedly haunted by a man who had shot himself in the basement. I didn't go down there but there was one take in which a shadowy figure could be seen lurking behind Trinity as she talked on the phone. It was a frightening night at dailies when that came up on screen. Larry and Andy wanted to use it in the film but the lawyers couldn't reach the spirit in time to get legal clearance.

Speaking of improbable postmortem appearances, if you believe Joey Pants, Cypher didn't really die in this scene and will be back for the sequels.

Scene 140: GOVERNMENT BUILDING. Another great acting scene. Hugo took this great speech by Agent Smith and made it even better. Like the pod sequence, this scene didn't change much from the first draft of the script to the last. It has to be one of the all time great film speeches. The city out the window is actually a huge photograph of Sydney, called a translite, with additional buildings strategically placed to block Sydney landmarks like the Harbor bridge. When we shot it, it was the largest translite ever made.

Scene 150: GOVERNMENT LOBBY. This scene took a very long time to shoot. Steve Courtley and Brian Cox, the special effects supervisors, had built about a hundred extra pillars and walls for this scene, and we used over half of them. If anything went wrong on a take, however, it took at least two hours to reset everything that was blown up. After each take, the air filled with toxic dust and we had to wear face masks while huge fans were brought in to clear the air. As a result, each take became like an Olympic event. The actors would be outside the set, pumping themselves up, knowing that they might only get one chance to get the action right. After a few days, everyone was convinced that there was nothing else to life except sitting around in this dingy warehouse waiting for pillars to be reset. This scene also contained two of the film's most difficult wire stunts, Trinity's flip off the wall and Neo's triple kick.

Scene 158: PILOT PROGRAM. A note for helicopter fanatics. Yes, we do realize that the actual helicopter is a B-212 but the graphic on Tank's screen is a B-206. Sorry about that.

Scene 164: HELICOPTER RESCUE. Any shot in this scene with the actors in it was shot on stage in front of a greenscreen while stuntmen performed the shots hanging from the helicopter as it weaves between buildings throughout Sydney. Shooting this scene was front page news on every station in Sydney the night it was shot.

Before it was shot, there were probably two months of meetings about what kind of glass would be used on the mini-building and how to get it to ripple. The whole scene was previsualized in CGI before it was shot. Eventually, John Gaeta and Steve Courtley sorted it all out.

Scenes 170, 172, 174, 176, 178: EL FIGHT. A set that it seemed we would never leave. I think this scene was originally scheduled for five days and ended up taking twelve or fifteen. The subway station was constructed over an outside railroad track. It was freezing cold and everyone got sick, making it particularly brutal for the actors. Every shot seemed like a struggle. It was hard while we were shooting but, in the end, the difficulty of the shoot made the final scene even more intense.

Scenes 204, 206, 208: SENTINEL ATTACK. These Sentinel scenes were strange shooting days because we had to plot the destruction for Sentinels that were to be added later. The Sentinel action had to be matched by John Gaeta during postproduction. So on the set, things ground to a standstill as Larry and Andy tried to plot out how a Sentinel would destroy the ship. At that point, it wasn't even entirely determined how exactly the Sentinels would move. It's a good thing they figured it out because, somehow, John Gaeta running up to Neo and Trinity's chair with a cube on a green stick is no substitute for the real thing. It looked good in the end but on the day, I think everyone's head was throbbing.

NOTE: Please see the larger, more comprehensive volume *The Art of The Matrix* (also published by Newmarket Press) for additional comments by Phil Oosterhouse on the storyboards and on excerpts from early drafts of *The Matrix* screenplay.

STILLS

NEO
Keanu Reeves

MORPHEUS
Laurence Fishburne

132

TRINITY
Carrie-Anne Moss

AGENT SMITH
Hugo Weaving

SWITCH, DOZER and TANK
Belinda McClory, Anthony Ray Parker, and Marcus Chong

CYPHER
Joe Pantoliano

AGENT BROWN (Paul Goddard), AGENT SMITH (Weaving),
and AGENT JONES (Robert Taylor)

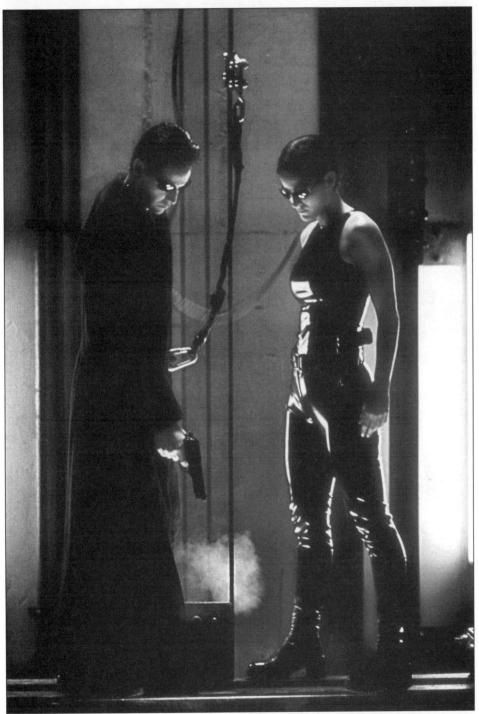

Neo and Trinity fight back

CAST AND CREW CREDITS

MATRIX

Written and Directed by LARRY and ANDY WACHOWSKI

Produced by . . . . JOEL SILVER

Executive Producers . . . . BARRIE M. OSBORNE
ANDREW MASON
ANDY WACHOWSKI
LARRY WACHOWSKI
ERWIN STOFF
BRUCE BERMAN
Director of Photography. . . . . BILL POPE
Production Designer. . . . . OWEN PATERSON
Editor . . . . ZACH STAENBERG
Costume Designer . . . . KYM BARRETT
Co-Producer. . . . . DAN CRACCHIOLO
Casting by . . . . MALI FINN C.S.A
SHAUNA WOLIFSON
Music Composed, Orchestrated
and Conducted by . . . . DON DAVIS
Visual Effects Supervisor . . . . JOHN GAETA

a WARNER BROS. presentation
in association with
VILLAGE ROADSHOW PICTURES -
GROUCHO II FILM PARTNERSHIP

a SILVER PICTURES production

Unit Production Manager . . . . CAROL HUGHES
1st Assistant Directors . . . . COLIN FLETCHER
JAMES McTEIGUE
2nd Assistant Directors . . . . NONI ROY
TOM READ
3rd Assistant Director . . . . PAUL SULLIVAN
Kung Fu Choreographer . . . . YUEN WO PING
Sound Designer/Supervising Sound Editor. . . . .
DANE A. DAVIS, MPSE
Conceptual Designer . . . . GEOFREY DARROW

CAST

Neo. KEANU REEVES
Morpheus . . . . LAURENCE FISHBURNE

Trinity . . . . CARRIE-ANNE MOSS
Agent Smith. . . . . HUGO WEAVING
Oracle . . . . GLORIA FOSTER
Cypher. . . . . JOE PANTOLIANO
Tank . . . . MARCUS CHONG
Apoc. . . . . JULIAN ARAHANGA
Mouse . . . . MATT DORAN
Switch . . . . BELINDA McCLORY
Dozer . . . . ANTHONY RAY PARKER
Agent Brown . . . . PAUL GODDARD
Agent Jones. . . . . ROBERT TAYLOR
Rhineheart . . . . DAVID ASTON
Choi . . . . MARC GRAY
Dujour. . . . . ADA NICODEMOU
Priestess . . . . DENI GORDON
Spoon Boy . . . . ROWAN WITT
Potentials. . . . . ELENOR WITT
TAMARA BROWN
JANAYA PENDER
ADRYN WHITE
NATALIE TJEN
Lieutenant . . . . BILL YOUNG
FedEx Man. . . . . DAVID O'CONNOR
Businessman. . . . . JEREMY BALL
Woman in Red . . . . FIONA JOHNSON
Old Man. . . . . HARRY LAWRENCE
Blind Man . . . . STEVE DODD
Security Guard. . . . . LUKE QUINTON
Guard . . . . LAWRENCE WOODWARD
Cop Who Captures Neo . . . . . . MICHAEL BUTCHER
Big Cop . . . . BERNIE LEDGER
Cops. . . . . ROBERT SIMPER
CHRIS SCOTT
Parking Cop . . . . NIGEL HARBACH
Helicopter Pilot . . . . MARTIN GRELIS
Stunt Coordinator . . . . GLENN BOSWELL
Assistant Stunt Coordinator . . . . PHIL MEACHAM

Stunt Doubles

Neo. . . . . CHAD STAHELSKI
DARKO TUSKAN
Neo/Agent Smith . . . . PAUL DOYLE

Trinity . . . . ANNETTE VAN MOORSEL	JACINTA LEONG
Morpheus . . . . ANDRE CHYNA McCOY	GODRIC COLE
Agent Brown. . . . . SHEA ADAMS	JUDITH HARVEY
Agent Jones. . . . . NIGEL HARBACH	ANDREW POWELL
Switch. . . . . GILLIAN STATHAM	DEBORAH RILEY
Cypher. . . . . BOB BOWLES	Set Decorators. . . . . TIM FERRIER
Mouse . . . . NASH EDGERTON	LISA 'BLITZ' BRENNAN

Trinity . . . . ANNETTE VAN MOORSEL
Morpheus . . . . ANDRE CHYNA McCOY
Agent Brown. . . . . SHEA ADAMS
Agent Jones. . . . . NIGEL HARBACH
Switch. . . . . GILLIAN STATHAM
Cypher. . . . . BOB BOWLES
Mouse . . . . NASH EDGERTON

Stunts

RAY ANTHONY	GREG BLANDY
RICHARD BOUE	SCOTT BREWER
DAVE BROWN	TODD BRYANT
MICHAEL CORRIGAN	HARRY DAKANALIS
DAR DAVIES	TERRY FLANAGAN
SCOTTY GREGORY	JOHNNY HALLYDAY
BRIAN ELLISON	LOU HORVATH
NIGEL KING	ALEX KISS
ALEX KUZELICIKI	IAN LIND
SCOTT McCLEAN	PHIL MEACHAM
CHRIS MITCHELL	TONY LYNCH
DARREN MITCHELL	STEVE MORRIS
BRETT PRAED	BAIT SOOBY
SOTIRI SOTIROPOULOS	GLENN SUTOR
BERNADETTE VAN GYEN	MARIJKE VAN GYEN
MICK VAN MOORSEL	WARWICK YOUNG

Hong Kong Kung Fu Team

YUEN Eagle SHUN YI	HUANG Sam KAI SEN
LAM Dion TAT HO	LEE Chew TAT CHIU
CHEN Tiger HU	LEUNG Madye SING HUNG
NILS BENDIX	DAXING ZHANG

Associate Producers . . . . RICHARD MIRISCH
CAROL HUGHES
Art Directors. . . . . HUGH BATEUP
MICHELLE McGAHEY
Assistant Art Directors . . . . JULES COOK
FIONA SCOTT
TONY WILLIAMS
Miniatures and Models Supervisor . . . . TOM DAVIES
Storyboard Artists . . . . STEVE SKROCE
TANI KUNITAKE
COLLIN GRANT
WARREN MANSER
Art Department Researcher. . . . . TARA KAMATH
Art Department Coordinator . . . . . TRISH FOREMAN
2D/3D Conceptual Designer . . . . . SERGEI CHADILOFF
Graphics . . . . KAREN HARBOROW
Illustrator . . . . PHIL SHEARER
Set Designers . . . . SARAH LIGHT

JACINTA LEONG
GODRIC COLE
JUDITH HARVEY
ANDREW POWELL
DEBORAH RILEY
Set Decorators. . . . . TIM FERRIER
LISA 'BLITZ' BRENNAN
MARTA McELROY
Script Supervisor. . . . . VICTORIA SULLIVAN
Camera Operator . . . . DAVID WILLIAMSON
Camera/Steadicam Operator . . . . . ROBERT AGGANIS
1st Assistant Camera . . . . DAVIA ELMES
2nd Assistant Camera. . . . . ADRIEN SEFFRIN
Stills Photographer . . . . JASON BOLAND
Sound Recordist. . . . . DAVID LEE
Boom Operators. . . . . JACK FRIEDMAN
GERRY NUCIFORA
Video Playback Operator . . . . MICHAEL TAYLOR
Property Master. . . . . LON LUCINI
Props . . . . MURRAY GOSSON
ADRIENNE OGLE
KATIE SHARROCK
Key Armourer. . . . . JOHN BOWRING
Action Vehicle Coordinators. . . . . JOHN ALLAN
TAPIO PIITULAINEN
Gaffer . . . . REG GARSIDE
Best Boy . . . . ALAN DUNSTAN
Rigger Gaffers . . . . CRAIG BRYANT
PAUL CUMMINGS
PAUL MOYES
STEVE JOHNSTON
MILES JONES
CHRIS LOVEDAY
KEN TALBOT
COLIN WYATT
Key Grip . . . . RAY BROWN
Head Grip . . . . IAN BIRD
Dolly Grips . . . . MICK VIVIAN
MAL BOOTH
GREG KING
ARON WALKER
Cam-Remote Operator . . . . PAUL MICALLEF
Rigging Grip . . . . DAVID BIRD
Standby Painters. . . . . TONY PILIOTIS
JON STILES
Special Effects Supervisors . . . . . . STEVE COURTLEY
BRIAN COX
Special Effects Coordinator . . . . . ROBINA OSBOURNE

139

Special Effects

RODNEY BURKE	MONTY FEIGUTH
DAVID PRIDE	ARTHUR SPINK JR
DAVE YOUNG	AARAN GORDON
RICHARD ALEXANDER	BRIAN BELCHER
NICK BERYK	JEFFREY BRIGGS
DARREN DE COSTA	PAUL FENN
LLOYD FINNEMORE	RAY FOWLER
BERNARD GOLENKO	DAVID GOLDIE
PAUL GORRIE	PAUL GREBERT
LEO HENRY	DAVID JAMES
JIM LENG	JUDY MAE LEWIS
SHANE MURPHY	JOHN NEAL
BRIGID OULSNAM	PETER OWENS
DANIEL PATMORE	GARRY PHILIPS
PIETER PLOOY	REECE ROBINSON
LOU STEFANEL	EDWIN TREASURE
THOMAS VAN KOEVERDEN	KERRY WILLIAMS
SOPHIE DICK	WALTER VAN VEENANDAAL

Key Makeup Artist . . . . NIKKI GOOLEY
Mr Fishburne's Makeup . . . . DEBORAH TAYLOR
Hairdresser . . . . CHERYL WILLIAMS
Assistant Makeup. . . . . SHERRY HUBBARD
Assistant Hairdresser . . . . SIMON ZANKER
Costume Supervisor . . . . LYN ASKEW
Costumers . . . . MARY LOU DA ROZA
ANDREA HOOD
ANDREW INFANTI
PAULINE WALKER
JENNY IRWIN
HELEN MATHER
NICK GODLEE
FIONA HOLLY
NICOLE BROWN
Hero Eye Wear Designed by. . . . . RICHARD WALKER
of BLIND OPTICS
Footwear Designed by . . . . AIRWALK
1st Assistant Editors . . . . PETER SKARRATT
CATHERINE CHASE (USA)
NOELLEEN WESTCOMBE (AUS)
Assistant Editors . . . . TOM COSTAIN
JENNIFER HICKS
JOHN LEE
BASIA OZERSKI
Visual Effects Editor . . . . KATE CROSSLEY
Assistant Visual Effects Editors . . . . . MARY E. WALTER
ALLEN CAPPUCCILLI
ELIZABETH MERCADO
Sound Effects Editors . . . . JULIA EVERSHADE
BRIC LINDEMANN
DAVID GRIMALDI
Dialogue Editors. . . . . CHARLES RITTER

SUSAN DUDECK
Supervising Foley Editor. . . . . THOM BRENNAN
Foley Editor . . . . VALERIE DAVIDSON
1st Assistant Sound Editor. . . . . NANCY BARKER
Assistant Sound Editors . . . . BARBARA DELPUECH
DAVID McCRELL
FRANK LONG
ADR Mixer . . . . TOM O'CONNELL
Foley Mixers . . . . MARYJO LANG
CAROLYN TAPP
Foley Artists . . . . JOHN ROESCH
HILDA HODGES
Re-Recording Mixers . . . . JOHN REITZ
GREGG RUDLOFF
DAVID CAMPBELL
2nd Stage . . . . KEVIN CARPENTER
Music Editors . . . . LORI ESCHLER FRYSTAK
ZIGMUND GRON
Music Score Recorded by. . . . . ARMIN STEINER
Music Score Mixed by . . . . LARRY MAH
Production Accountant . . . . MARGE ROWLAND
Production Accountant - Australia . . . ALISTAIR JENKINS
1st Assistant Accountant. . . . . MANDY BUTLER
Assistant Accountant . . . . MICHELE D'ARCEY
Locations Manager . . . . PETER LAWLESS
Production Coordinator . . . . MEGAN WORTHY
Assistant Production Coordinator . . KATHERINE GAMBLE
Production Secretary . . . . JUSTINE VOLLMER
Hong Kong Kung Fu Coordinator . . . . CAROL KIM
Assistant to the Wachowski Brothers PHIL OOSTERHOUSE
Assistant to Joel Silver . . . . MICHELLE TUELLA
Assistants to Barrie M. Osborne. . . . . ANNIE GILHOOLY
ANGELA PRITCHARD
Assistant to Andrew Mason. . . . . EMMA JACOBS
Assistant to Dan Cracchiolo . . . . ROB POLGAR
Assistant to Mr. Reeves . . REINALDO PUENTES-TUCKI
Assistant to Mr. Fishburne . . . . SANDRA HODGE
Australian Casting . . . . MULLINARS CASTING
Extras Casting . . . . TIM LITTLETON
Dialect Coach . . . . SUZANNE CELESTE
Physical Trainers. . . . . DENISE SNYDER
MICHELLE ROWE
Cast Sports Masseur . . . . 'LONGY' NGUYIN
Medical Advisors . . . . DR. IAN I.T. ARMSTRONG, M.D.
DR. JOSEPH M. HORRIGAN, D.C.
Publicist . . . . FIONA SEARSON
Safety Coordinator . . . . LAWRENCE WOODWARD
Saftey Officers . . . . SPIKE CHERRIE
KERRY BLAKEMAN
Nurse. . . . . JACQUIE ROBERTSON
Unit Manager . . . . WILL MATTHEWS

Assistant Unit Manager . . . . . . GRAYDEN LE BRETON	Camera Helicopter Pilot . . . . GARY TICEHURST
Construction Supervisor. . . . . PHIL WORTH	Aerial Coordinator . . . . TERRY LEE
Construction Coordinator . . . . MARIANNE EVANS	Underwater Camera Operator . . ROGER BUCKINGHAM
Scenic Artist . . . . PETER COLLIAS	Wescom Operator . . . . PHIL PASTAHOV
Construction. . . . . JOHN PICKERING	

Construction:
ANDREW STAIG
MARCUS SMITH
TONY BARDOLPH
BRETT BARTLETT
MARK GATT
TERENCE LORD
WAYNE PORTER
JOHN REGA
TREVOR SMITH

Caterers . . . . KEVIN VARNES
KERRY FETZER
GUY FIRTH

Makeup Special Effects Designed and Created by BOB McCARRON S.M.A

Senior Makeup SPFX Artist . . . . . WENDY SAINSBURY
Makeup SPFX Artists . . . . RICK CONNELLY
	SONJA SMUK
	ELKA WARDEGA

Animatronic Prosthetics Created by MAKEUP EFFECTS GROUP STUDIO

PAUL KATTE	NICK NICOLAOU

Animatronics Designer . . . . TREVOR TIGHE
Screen Graphics Coordinator . . . . . ADAM McCULLOCH
Screen Graphics Assistant. . . . . SAMI MacKENZIE-KERR
AMX Programmer . . . . JOHN TURNER

2nd Unit

Director. . . . . BRUCE HUNT
Director of Photography. . . . . ROSS EMERY
1st Assistant Director . . . . TOBY PEASE
Production Coordinators . . . . JANE GRIFFIN
	JULIA PETERS
1st Assistant Camera. . . . . FRANK FLICK
Gaffer . . . . PAUL JOHNSTONE
Best Boy . . . . ROBBIE BURR
Key Grip . . . . TOBY COPPING
Dolly Grip . . . . BEN HYDE
Script Supervisor. . . . . GILLIAN STEINE
Video Operator. . . . . ANTHONY TOY
Locations Manager . . . . ROBIN CLIFTON
Props . . . . JAMES COX
	JAKE CLIFTON
	SHANE BENNETT
Makeup Artist . . . . KATHY COURTNEY
Wardrobe. . . . . FIONA NICHOLLS
Unit Manager. . . . . SIMON LUCAS
Assistant Unit Manager . . . . DICK BECKETT
Production Secretary . . . . LIZZIE EVES
2nd Assistant Director . . . . JEREMY SEDLEY
Production Aide. . . . . BELINDA DEAN
Special Effects . . . . KIMBLE HILDER
	PATRICK CARMIGGELT
Safety Officer. . . . . BRIAN ELLISON
Nurse . . . . HELEN COX
Caterers . . . . JOHN FAITHFUL
	JULIE-ANNE LINCOLN
Picture Helicopter Pilot . . . . GREG DUNCOMBE

Production Aides

NATHAN ANDERSON	SASSICA DONOHOO
MARCUS DWYER	JUAN GOLDSMITH
MARVIN HAYES	MELISSA JOHNSTON
ALEX KAUFMAN	

Staff Assistants

PETER FORBES	JAYNE JOHNSON
TOMMY O'REILLY	DANIELLE OSBORNE
JANET SEPPELT	BRYCE TIBBEY
CHRIS WHITTLE	SINCLAIR WHALLEY
CHARLY WRENCHER	LUKE WRENCHER
MARK FLETCHER	MICHAEL ROTH
SUZANNE MIDDLETON	JANE HEALY
SALLY SHARPE	DONNA HUDDLESTON
BIANCA HAVAS	LEA LENNON
FIONA LANDRETH	BELINDA LOWSON

Visual Effects Producer . . . . MATT FERRO

MANEX VISUAL EFFECTS, LLC.

Associate VFX Supervisor . . . . JANEK SIRRS
VFX Producer . . . . ALLISOUN F. LAMB
Digital FX Producer . . . . DIANA GIORGIUTTI
Digital FX Supervisor. . . . . RODNEY IWASHINA
Technology Supervisor. . . . . KIM LIBRERI
Digital Line Producer . . . . JEREMY BEADELL

Line Producer . . . . PAUL TAGLIANETTI
Production Aide. . . . . MAUREEN BLUME
Assistant Digital Coordinator . . . . . . NOAH MIZRAHI
Production Aide - Aus . . . . HOLLY RADCLIFFE
Science Officer . . . . DAN PIPONI
Software Development. . . . . JEREMY YARBROW
Lead Color and Lighting TD . . . . RUDY POAT
Lead Shader Writer . . . . STEVE DEMERS
Lead Tec Supervisor . . . . IVO KOS
Compositer/Painter . . . . AMANDA EVANS
CG Designer/Animator . . . . GRANT NIESNER
FX Animator . . . . AL ARTHUR
Pre-Viz Animator - Aus. . . . . NICO GREY
3D Texture Animator . . . . BRENT HARTSHORN
Texture Painter. . . . . DEVORAH PETTY
2D Paint/Roto . . . . JEFF ALLEN
2D/3D Paint . . . . JAY JOHNSON
Conceptual Art. . . . . STEVE BURG
Matte Painting . . . . CHARLES DARBY
Systems Manager. . . . . MARTIN WEAVER
Systems Administrator . . . . CHARLES HENRICH
Systems Support . . . . VICTOR E. VALE IV
DEBORAH THOMAS
MARK BURNS
Editors . . . . ROY BERKOWITZ
ANTHONY MARK
BRIAN PORTER
Film Recorder . . . . GREG SHIMP
Character Animators . . . . MATT FARELL
JAMIE PILGRIM
JOHN LEE
ANDREW SCHNEIDER
MICHAEL FFISHHEMSCHOOT
Animators/Modelers . . . . DANIEL KLEM
SEAN WHITE
ENRIQUE VILA
Technical Supervisors . . . . JOHN VOLNY
JOSEPH LITTLEJOHN
LEWIS SIEGEL
JASON WARDLE
GIL BARON
MICHAEL McNEILL
SOPHIA S. LONGORIA
JOHN A. TISSAVARY
Compositors. . . . . BARNEY ROBSON
JOHN P. NUGENT
MARY LETZ
LAURA HANIGAN
DANIEL P. ROSEN

Bullet Time

R&D/Tech Supervisor . . . . . . GEORGE BORSHUKOV
Character Animator . . . . GERARD BENJAMIN PIERRE
Tech Consultant. . . . . MARK WEINGARTNER
Pre-Viz Animator . . . . ROB NUNN
Research and Development . . . . BILL COLLIS
2D Animator . . . . ART DAVID
Animator. . . . . DANIEL SUNWOOD
Compositors. . . . . JOHN F. SASAKI
J. D. COWLES
THOMAS PROCTOR
Technicians . . . . PAUL CLEMENTE
FRANK GALLEGO
DAVID NUNEZ
Sokkia Survey Crew . . . . KIRK BOLTE
ANDREW BORSCZ

DFILM SERVICES

Executive Producer . . . . PETER DOYLE
Digital Effects Supervisor. . . . . JOHN THUM
Digital Effects Producer . . . . ALARIC McAUSLAND
Computer Animation Supervisor . . . . SALLY GOLDBERG
Animation Supervisor . . . . IAN McGUFFIE
Editorial Supervisor. . . . . JAN MACGUIRE
Editor Assistant. . . . . NATACHA TEDESCHI
Technology Manager. . . . . PAUL RYAN
Production Coordinator . . . . REBECCA FOX
Digital Composite Supervisors . . . . TIM CROSBIE
MARK NETTLETON
Digital Compositors . . . . STEPHEN LUNN
DAVID HODSON
Rotoscope Artists . . . . ELIZABETH CARLON
VANESSA WHITE
CGI Lead Animators . . . . DOMINIC PARKER
DANIELE COLAJACOMO
CGI Animators. . . . . JUSTIN MARTIN
RANGI SUTTON

ANIMAL LOGIC FILM

VFX Supervisor . . . . LYNNE CARTWRIGHT
CGI Artist/Colorist. . . . . DAVID DULAC
Programmer . . . . JUSTEN MARSHALL
CGI Designer. . . . . JANE MILLEDGE
System Admin . . . . RON KORPI
CGI Artists . . . . LINDSAY FLEAY
ANDREW QUINN
BEN GUNSBERGER
Inferno Artists . . . . KIRSTY MILLAR
JOHN BRESLIN

ROBIN CAVE
KRISTA JORDAN
Compositors . . . . CHARLIE ARMSTRONG
GRANT EVERETT
MARYANNE LAURIC
Producer . . . . ZAREH NALBANDIAN
Production Aide . . . . EDWEANA WENKART
I/O Supervisor . . . . NAOMI HATCHMAN
Screen Graphics . . . . THOMAS KAYSER

Additional Visual Effects . . . . ALMALGAMATED PIXELS
Color Timer. . . . . DAVID ORR
Negative Cutter . . . . MO HENRY
Titles Designed by . . . . GREENBERG/SCHLUTER
Titles and Optics by . . . . PACIFIC TITLE/MIRAGE
Soundtrack Album on MAVERICK RECORDS

"DISSOLVED GIRL"
Written by
ROBERT DEL NAJA, GRANTLEY MARSHALL,
ANDREW VOWLES, SARA J. AND MATT SCHWARTZ
Performed by MASSIVE ATTACK
Courtesy of VIRGIN RECORDS LTD.
by Arrangement with VIRGIN RECORDS AMERICA, INC.

"DRAGULA (HOT ROD HERMAN MIX)"
Written by ROB ZOMBIE and SCOTT HUMPHREY
Performed by ROB ZOMBIE
Courtesy of GEFFEN RECORDS
Under License from
UNIVERSAL MUSIC SPECIAL MARKETS

"MINDFIELDS"
Written by LIAM HOWLETT
Performed by PRODIGY
Courtesy of MAVERICK RECORDING COMPANY/
XL RECORDINGS/BEGGAR'S BANQUET
By Arrangement with WARNER SPECIAL PRODUCTS

"LEAVE YOU FAR BEHIND
(LUNATICS ROLLER COASTER MIX)"
Written by
SIMON SHACKLETON and HOWARD SAUNDERS
Performed by LUNATIC CALM
Courtesy of UNIVERSAL MUSIC (UK) LTD.
Under License from
UNIVERSAL MUSIC SPECIAL MARKETS

"CLUBBED TO DEATH (KURAYAMINO MIX)"
Written by ROB DOUGAN

Performed by ROB D
Courtesy of A&M RECORDS LIMITED/
UNIVERSAL-ISLAND RECORDS
Under License from
UNIVERSAL MUSIC SPECIAL MARKETS

"PRIME AUDIO SOUP"
Written by JACK DANGERS and C.DODD
Performed by MEAT BEAT MANIFESTO
Courtesy of NOTHING RECORDS
& PLAY IT AGAIN SAM/HEARTBEAT RECORDS
Under License from
UNIVERSAL MUSIC SPECIAL MARKETS

"MINOR SWING"
Written by DJANGO REINHARDT
and STEPHANE GRAPPELLI
Performed by DJANGO REINHARDT
Courtesy of THE RCA RECORDS
LABEL OF BMG ENTERTAINMENT
"BEGIN THE RUN"
FROM "NIGHT OF THE LEPUS"
Written by JAMIE HASKELL

"I'M BEGINNING TO SEE THE LIGHT"
Written by
DUKE ELLINGTON, DON GEORGE,
JOHNNY HODGES and HARRY JAMES
Performed by DUKE ELLINGTON
Courtesy of THE RCA RECORDS
LABEL OF BMG ENTERTAINMENT

"SPYBREAK!"
Written by ALEX GIFFORD
Performed by PROPELLERHEADS
Courtesy of
DREAMWORKS RECORDS/WALL OF SOUND
Under License from
UNIVERSAL MUSIC SPECIAL MARKETS/
PROPELLERHEADS

"WAKE UP"
Written by
ZACK DE LA ROCHA, BRAD WILK,
TIM COMMERFORED and TOM MORELLO
Performed by RAGE AGAINST THE MACHINE
Courtesy of EPIC RECORDS
By Arrangement with
SONY MUSIC LICENSING

"ROCK IS DEAD"
Written by MARILYN MANSON,
TWIGGY RAMIREZ and MADONNA WAYNE GACY
Performed by MARILYN MANSON
Courtesy of NOTHING/INTERSCOPE RECORDS
Under License from
UNIVERSAL MUSIC SPECIAL MARKETS

Cinematography by SIMON CAROL ARCHIVE

The Prisoner Clip provided by POLYGRAM FILMED
ENTERTAINMENT

The Producers wish to thank the following
THE CITY OF SYDNEY COUNCIL
THE NSW PREMIER'S DEPARTMENT
THE NSW FILM & TELEVISION OFFICE
CASA
THE MARITIME CENTRE, SYDNEY
STREETLIGHTS PROGRAM
AMX

Filmed on location in SYDNEY, AUSTRALIA
and at FOX STUDIOS AUSTRALIA

Filmed with PANAVISION® Camera and Lenses

Color by ATLAB AUSTRALIA

Prints by TECHNICOLOR®

KODAK Motion Picture Products

DOLBY DIGITAL in selected Theatres

DIGITAL DTS SOUND in selected Theatres

SONY DYNAMIC DIGITAL SOUND in selected Theatres

THE MATRIX

www.whatisthematrix.com
password: steak

THE ART OF THE MATRIX

Screenplay and art by Larry & Andy Wachowski. Storyboards, conceptual art, and commentaries by Steve Skroce, Geof Darrow, Tani Kunitake, Warren Manser, and Collin Grant. Introduction by Zach Staenberg. Scene notes by Phil Oosterhouse. Afterword by William Gibson. Edited by Spencer Lamm.

"From the Wachowski Brothers' stick figures, to 700 scene-by-scene storyboards, to conceptual art, it's all in here, including scenes that were never filmed for safety or budgetary reasons, as well as the shooting script and ten pages of script notes and deleted scenes from the script..."
—*Creative Screenwriting*

"A stunning document of a stunning film."
—*Minneapolis Star-Tribune*

"This pictorial feast is a must-have for science-fiction fans and *Matrix* loyalists.... "
—*Publishers Weekly*

"[A] wonderland of conceptual drawings, storyboards and cut scenes from the sci-fi blockbuster....This tome reveals far more than the *Matrix* DVD does about the clarity of the vision of writer-directors Andy and Larry Wachowski.... Film buffs who are still asking 'What is the Matrix?' will learn more from these pages than Morpheus could ever tell."
—*Entertainment Weekly*

"Beautifully designed and doorstop-heavy, *The Art of The Matrix* offers insights into the imaginations that spawned the milestone film. It's the sort of book you can just open at random and be wowed by."
—*Premiere*

THIS UNIQUE VOLUME INCLUDES:

- The shooting script by writers/directors Larry and Andy Wachowski
- Black & white storyboards (600+) by Steve Skroce
- Color storyboards by Tani Kunitake and Collin Grant
- Color renderings and conceptual drawings by Geof Darrow, presented in four double-sided gatefolds
- Conceptuals by Warren Manser
- 32-page color album of stills and posters

- Three storyboard sequences cut before filming
- Commentary by the artists about their work on the film, interviewed especially for this book
- Thumbnail sketches by the Wachowski Brothers
- Intro. by Zach Staenberg, Oscar®-winning Film Editor
- Scene notes by Phil Oosterhouse
- Deleted script excerpts
- Film credits

---

488 pages plus gatefolds. 8³/₈" x 10⁷/₈".
Over 1000 illustrations.
Four-color printing throughout.
1-55704-405-8. $60.00. Hardcover.

Order from your local bookstore or from Newmarket Press, 18 East 48 Street, New York, NY 10017; Tel (212) 832-3575 or (800) 669-3903; Fax (212) 832-3629; e-mail mailbox@newmarketpress.com; www.newmarketpress.com